To get more information on Process Synchronization, Value Mapping™, and Pipeline Radar™, plus additional insights on implementing the ideas in this book, please visit my web site at www.web2one.com or send me an email at bobs@web2one.com

Cascading Need Phenomenon
What initially appears to be one business problem or requirement is actually a compendium of many sub-problems and requirements impacting many different Stakeholders in an organization in different ways.

Complete Value Proposition
Combination of a value statement along with proof and validation of the value, how that value is actually created and quantified, and how that solution is differentiated to deliver more value than its competition.

Content Conundrum
Phenomenon where the Total Cost of Content goes up while the average value of that content to the selling process goes down.

Core Intellectual Assets
A company's intellectual property has two components that should be managed. The first component includes the facts, insights, and opinions (raw materials) that make up the foundation for a company's Complete Value Propositions and best sales practices. The second component includes the Sanctioned Content (finished goods) that reflects those raw materials knowledge assets.

Critical Communications Activities
A company's branding programs, lead generation activities, and selling interactions including sales and sales support calls, as well as follow-up correspondence.

Customer Message Management (CMM)
A broad-based marketing and sales effectiveness strategy for content and communications. CMM includes processes and best practices that help companies focus more on their customers' needs so they improve and harden their value propositions, create more sales-ready content and tools, and enable their sales channels to have more relevant and effective conversations with prospects and customers.

Event Horizon
The point of no return in a Black Hole where time and space begin to warp and things never escape. In this book it refers to the front end of the marketing and selling process where tremendous waste and inefficiencies exist, and where time, effort, money, and opportunities are lost because of marketing and sales misalignment.

Inside-Out
The process of viewing the world primarily from a product perspective.

Internal Champions
People inside customer and prospect organizations that assist sales people in delivering the message and helping them convince other Stakeholders to buy a product or service.

Morphing

When sales and sales-support people modify Sanctioned Content, especially presentation content.

Outside-In

The process of viewing the world from the customer's perspective.

Pipeline Radar™

The process of measuring and visually graphing changes in sales pipeline behavior over time, including the size, shape, flow, and turbulence of the sales opportunities in that pipeline.

Process Synchronization

A best practice of formally integrating the marketing and selling processes and aligning this integrated process with the way customers buy.

Sanctioned Content

A company's approved sales support content and marketing collateral.

Smart Taxonomy

The ability to use the Value Mapping knowledge base as the primary index for marketing and sales content. This allows sales people to find just the right information in the context of the person they are talking to and what that person's specific requirements and needs are.

Stakeholders

People in prospect and customer organizations who are part of, or who can impact the buying process for, a product or service because they have a stake in the result.

Total Cost of Content

Combination of the visible costs of creating and managing Sanctioned Content plus all the different invisible costs of morphing and using the sanctioned content as the volume of content grows.

Value DNA

The many facts, insights, and opinions that combine to make up Complete Value Propositions.

Value Mapping™

New best practice that requires companies to systematically document all the ways their products and services deliver value to the different Stakeholders they sell to, resulting in a knowledge base that maps the messages, provides just-in-time sales coaching, and becomes the DNA for everything marketing and sales organizations produce and do on a day-to-day basis.

Web-Assisted Selling

Aggressively exploiting web conferencing throughout the sales process to reduce selling costs and improve sales effectiveness.

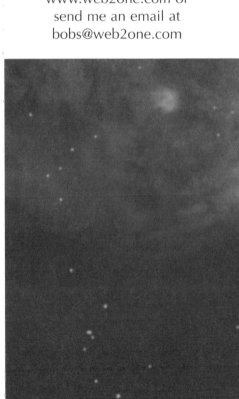

To get more information on Process Synchronization, Value Mapping™, and Pipeline Radar™, plus additional insights on implementing the ideas in this book, please visit my web site at www.web2one.com or send me an email at bobs@web2one.com

Escaping the Black Hole: Minimizing the Damage from the Marketing-Sales Disconnect

ESCAPING THE BLACK HOLE:
MINIMIZING THE DAMAGE FROM THE MARKETING-SALES DISCONNECT

Robert J. Schmonsees

Australia · Canada · Mexico · Singapore · Spain · United Kingdom · United States

THOMSON

™

SOUTH-WESTERN

Escaping the Black Hole: Minimizing the Damage from the Marketing-Sales Disconnect
Robert J. Schmonsees

COPYRIGHT © 2005 by Texere, an imprint of Thomson/South-Western, a part of The Thomson Corporation. Thomson and the Star logo are trademarks used herein under license.

Composed by: *Interactive Composition Corporation*

Printed in the United States of America by: RR Donnelley & Sons, Company–Crawfordsville
1 2 3 4 5 08 07 06 05
This book is printed on acid-free paper.

ISBN: 0-324-30125-1

Library of Congress Cataloging in Publication Number is available. See page 213 for details.

For more information about our products, contact us at:

Thomson Learning Academic Resource Center 1-800-423-0563

Thomson Higher Education
5191 Natorp Boulevard
Mason, Ohio 45040
USA

Asia (including India)
Thomson Learning
5 Shenton Way
#01-01 UIC Building
Singapore 068808

Australia/New Zealand
Thomson Learning Australia
102 Dodds Street
Southbank, Victoria 3006
Australia

Canada
Thomson Nelson
1120 Birchmount Road
Toronto, Ontario
M1K 5G4
Canada

Latin America
Thomson Learning
Seneca, 53
Colonia Polanco
11560 Mexico
D. F. Mexico

UK/Europe/Middle East/Africa
Thomson Learning
High Holborn House
50/51 Bedford Row
London WC1R 4LR
United Kingdom

Spain (including Portugal)
Thomson Paraninfo
Calle Magallanes, 25
28015 Madrid, Spain

To my parents, who taught me that anything is possible,
and to my wife Judy, who always helps me believe it.

Table of Contents

FOREWORD: ix

INTRODUCTION: xiii

PART I

DISCOVERING THE EVENT HORIZON

CHAPTER 1: *The Schwarzschild Radius* 3

CHAPTER 2: *The Increasing Market Complexity* 12

CHAPTER 3: *The Changing Market Dynamics* 21

CHAPTER 4: *The Changing Communications Model* 27

CHAPTER 5: *Understanding the Disconnect* 37

CHAPTER 6: *Strategic Mistakes* 52

CHAPTER 7: *Missed Opportunities* 62

PART II

CLOSING THE GAP

CHAPTER 8: *Alignment as a Core Strategy* 83

CHAPTER 9: *Conceptualizing the Ecosystem* 91

CHAPTER 10: *Discovering the Holy Grail* 96

CHAPTER 11: *Enabling the Ecosystem* 110

PART III

IMPLEMENTING THE BUYER-CENTRIC REVENUE MODEL

CHAPTER 12: *Understanding the Model* 115

CHAPTER 13: *Integrated Pipeline Management* 121

PART IV

IMPLEMENTING THE VALUE-CENTRIC COMMUNICATIONS MODEL

CHAPTER 14: *Understanding the Model*   139

CHAPTER 15: *Adopting the VCCM*   145

CHAPTER 16: *Building a Value Map*   151

CHAPTER 17: *Optimizing the Sanctioned Content*   161

CONCLUSION: *The Opportunity for Marketing*   195

INDEX 203

Foreword

*E*SCAPING THE BLACK HOLE is about pushing the edge of the envelope with new ideas and processes. Some are tactical, some are strategic, and a few are truly revolutionary. Its promise is a clear and concise blueprint for creating a highly effective and more synchronized sales and marketing ecosystem.

I admit this is a daunting challenge. Like many sales executives, I had embraced the notion that marketing people could never understand what goes on in the customer's mind. Marketing's approach was just too different from sales. I know very few companies that have sales and marketing working together, where all parts are synchronized and implanted in an "ecologically healthy" corporate culture. In many companies, sales and marketing departments have grown apart because too many projects were designed to satisfy the egos of the leaders rather than to delight the company's customers.

When I think of the disconnect between sales and marketing, I think of a cacaphony of noise. When marketing sees an opportunity, they tend to commission a composer to write a symphony that will attract a wide audience. Like classical music, marketing evokes a predictable stream of predictable emotions. When salespeople see a customer, on the other hand, they hear anything but a symphony. The world of selling is more like jazz, the art of the moment. Salespeople listen to a customer's riff for a while, and then respond with a riff of their own. Good salespeople are masters at improvisation.

Bob's view is a little different. He sees selling and marketing as an integrated, multi-dimensional challenge that involves maximizing the transfer of knowledge between marketing, sales, partners, customers, and prospects through simple, systematic processes that help marketing and sales professionals see the world from the outside-in.

I have known Bob Schmonsees for many years, and have admired his relentless passion for getting sales and marketing to listen to the customer's tune and for continually driving the creation of "customer-centric" organizations. Bob has directed several sales and marketing teams and suffered the indignities that come with premature and poorly planned product launches, ineffective marketing messages, and misinformed salespeople. As the CEO of several software companies, he's been ahead of the curve, set the bar to the highest level, enjoyed great success, and also experienced the agony of failure. Bob and I have engaged in many lengthy discussions over the last dozen years on how to best create a coordinated and symbiotic sales and marketing team that is truly driven by the needs of the customer.

Bob has done a little more intellectual weightlifting than others in the field, and he has discovered a simple process for creating and hardening a company's value propositions. Here is where Bob's genius lies. His battle cry is "value . . . as the customer defines it," and his weapons are powerful and precise. Bob's patented methodology called "Value Mapping" forces sales and marketing to take a closer look at their customers' business problems and begin a systematic discovery and knowledge-transfer process that helps everybody from the CEO to the salesperson articulate the value proposition in a way that is consistent, objective, and measurable.

Value creation is the heart of any business, and Value Mapping lets you create a visual map of your company's "Value DNA," and provide your salespeople with just-in-time coaching on all the different elements of your value propositions so that they are as crystal clear as a mountain lake. This is truly a revolutionary process, which in my view will become as important to marketing as forecasting is to sales. Value Mapping quickly raises customer knowledge up the organizational flagpole, and allows sales and marketing to synchronize their efforts arround the precise value that their solutions deliver to the marketplace.

Value Mapping is just one of the innovative new processes and best practices in this book that will help B-to-B companies avoid what Bob calls "The Black Hole," that powerful energy field that absorbs countless dumptrucks filled with useless marketing material along with millions of dollars of wasted sales efforts.

Bob is a realist, however. He understands that creating a Synchronized Marketing and Sales Ecosystem may be simple to talk about and understand, but is not quite as easy to achieve. People resist change. But what's the alternative? Irrelevance!

The bottom line is that the new ideas in this book will help you stop talking about customer-centricity and help you actually begin to walk the walk. And that is what effective marketing and selling is all about.

—Gerhard Gschwandtner
  Publisher and Founder
  Selling Power Magazine
  Fredericksburg, Virginia

Introduction

"The 1990s are so over, they never happened."

—MICHAEL HAMMER.[1]

THERE IS A MARKETING AND SALES EFFECTIVENESS and execution crisis facing companies that sell complex products and services. The marketing and selling costs in many companies are growing faster than revenues, and as the twenty-first century economy evolves, business-to-business (B-to-B) marketing and sales executives face some hard realities:

- More than 50 percent of salespeople are not achieving their sales quotas.[2]
- More than 75 percent of new product launches fail to meet initial expectations.[3]
- At least 90 percent of sales opportunities don't close as forecasted.[4]

It's become all too convenient to blame the current business economy for these statistics. Sure, budgets have been cut and there are fewer opportunities to chase, but that's not the whole story. It is the thesis of this book that too many marketing and sales executives were asleep at the switch during the last two decades when it came to increasing marketing and sales alignment and effectiveness. As a result, marketing and sales organizations have become increasingly disconnected and dysfunctional.

---

[1]Michael Hammer, *The Agenda* (New York: Crown Business/Random House, 2001).

[2]Barry Trailer and Jim Dickie, "Sales Effectiveness Insights," executive white paper published by CSO Insights (2004): 2.

[3]Steve Sarno, Alston Gardner, and Jay Klompmaker, "Impact Marketing Research: Winning the Product Launch," research published by the University of North Carolina (2000).

[4]Barry Trailer and Jim Dickie, "Sales Effectiveness Insights," executive white paper published by CSO Insights (2004): 3.

I have always had a passion for the marketing and sales process, and have read every book I could get my hands on about the subject. Unfortunately, most of these books concentrated on marketing tactics, sales management techniques, or proprietary selling methodologies. While they all have some good ideas, I couldn't find a single one that focused on reducing the significant amount of waste, cost, and lost revenue caused by the disconnect between marketing and sales organizations.

So a few years ago, after shutting down a high-tech start-up, I started to read what eventually ended up being several hundred articles, studies, and white papers on marketing and sales effectiveness. I also began conducting detailed interviews with the executives of more than 250 companies to find out what they were doing to improve marketing and sales productivity.

What I discovered from this process was that the marketing and sales model was severely broken in a lot of B-to-B companies, and it didn't just break overnight in 2000 when the economy went south and the markets had a meltdown. In the last twenty years or so, a lot of marketing and sales executives made some strategic mistakes and missed several golden opportunities to improve both the alignment and effectiveness of their respective organizations. As a result, the gap between marketing and sales actually grew wider, injecting additional waste and inefficiencies into the go-to-market model, and the percentage of marketing and sales expenses to revenue in many companies increased dramatically.

Unfortunately, the effects of the marketing and sales disconnect went virtually unnoticed during the thriving economy of the 1990s when almost everyone was making their numbers. The game has changed, however, and now there are a lot of dysfunctional marketing and sales organizations in which opportunities are routinely lost and a significant amount of cost, time, and resources are consumed by a phenomenon I call the "B-to-B Black Hole."

GETTING LUCKY EARLY

I got my first sales job in 1969, and have been managing high-tech B-to-B marketing and sales organizations since 1975. I've had more than my share of successes and failures, worked with some great products and some duds, and, truth be told, made most of the exact same management mistakes chronicled in this book. I've also had the good fortune over the years to work with some of the best marketing and sales minds in a wide range of industries, in all phases of the business life cycle, from start-ups to some of the brand leaders in the Fortune 100.

I had some lucky breaks early on in my career that established my fundamental beliefs about marketing and sales. My first stroke of luck was actually a job rejection. I majored in English in college, and after a pretty successful football—but less than stellar academic—career, I was recruited by Aetna Insurance as a sales trainee. I had progressed through a series of increasingly intense interviews, and was scheduled for my final meeting with the VP of the division. Unfortunately, I wore a pink shirt and a double-breasted suit to the interview. Remember, this was 1969, and the VP took one look at me and said, "Son, I don't think you're Aetna material."

Luckily, I also had an interview scheduled with the local IBM office later that day. After changing into a different suit and white shirt, I met with the branch manager who asked me to take what was called the Programmer's Aptitude Test (PAT).

I thought I was a goner because tests were never my strong point and I had never even seen a computer, other than on television. For some unknown reason, however, the PAT indicated I had the skill sets IBM was looking for. They made me a job offer, and I went to work for one of the most effective and best-aligned marketing and sales organizations in the world at that time.

The second lucky break came a few years later when a computer time-sharing company recruited me away from IBM. During the next two years, I became this company's top salesperson, and was promoted to marketing director at the age of 25. The move from salesperson to marketing management resulted in a 50 percent cut in income, but I jumped at the opportunity anyway. As a result, I saw the different aspects of the marketing and sales-support side of the business, through which I discovered the difficulties in dealing with the demands of salespeople.

By the late 1970s I had become the chief marketing and sales officer for a publicly traded software and service company. During this time I began to implement some crude sales automation processes like lead tracking, pipeline management, and forecasting, long before they became common-place. This unfettered access to the latest technology throughout my career has given me a unique perspective on marketing and sales automation. As you will see in later chapters, I believe we are just beginning to exploit many of the computer and communications technologies available for improving B-to-B marketing and sales effectiveness.

THE UNLUCKY BREAK

In January of 1984, I was standing in the wrong place at the wrong time. I was hit by an out-of-control skier and was permanently paralyzed from the waist down.

After four months of rigorous rehabilitation, I tried to go back to my old job as the VP of marketing and sales. While my employer and coworkers were extremely supportive throughout my rehabilitation, there was a clear difference between our perceptions of how my disability would affect my performance. Sure, there were additional challenges with travel, but I felt I was the exact same person I was before the accident, only a little bit shorter and with wheels. They, however, saw me as this poor fellow who was a shadow of his former self, and I think it made a lot of them uncomfortable.

As a result, I made the decision to go it alone. I spent the next five years working with, and investing in, over a dozen high-tech start-ups, some of which were really breaking new ground. This included short-term operational and advisory engagements as:

- The chief marketing and sales officer for a start-up company that developed one of the first computer-based mapping and vehicle routing systems almost twenty years before things like Hertz's™ Never Lost™.
- The CEO of one of the first companies to develop and market sales automation software at a time when most companies were wondering why a salesperson would ever need a computer.
- A marketing and strategy consultant to one of the few artificial intelligence companies that actually made it, as well as one of the first companies to successfully sell enterprise-class computer software over the telephone.

These experiences helped me appreciate the importance of marketing and sales alignment, especially when it comes to communicating new ideas and successfully launching new products.

In 1988 I decided I wanted to get back to running a more substantial marketing and sales organization. I quickly found out, however, that my wheelchair was still a larger issue in most people's eyes than it was in mine. As a result, I had to scale back my expectations and start over from the ground up. After a few months, I finally ended up accepting a first-line sales management job in a mid-sized enterprise software company.

But then I got lucky again! This company started to flounder, and it became clear to the CEO and the board that they needed some new vision and direction. I convinced them we needed to put all the activities that touched the customer under a single executive and create what many companies are now calling a Chief Customer Officer. Two months later I was promoted a couple of levels to the VP of marketing, sales, and customer service. During the ten months I had spent as a front-line sales manager, however, I got to see some of the marketing and sales disconnects from the trenches. I also participated in lots of sales calls, and I learned firsthand how much more sophisticated and cunning prospects had become in their buying tactics since my days carrying a bag.

THE WISDOMWARE EXPERIENCE

I continued to run global marketing and sales organizations for the next seven years, and in 1996 decided to form my own company called WisdomWare to address the sales effectiveness problem with a new type of sales coaching software. I was able to attract a small amount of venture funding, and we released the first version of the product in 1998.

WisdomWare's vision was truly unique at the time, and like a lot of new ideas, it really pushed the technology envelope. I had never before been associated with a product concept that generated so much initial excitement in both senior executives and salespeople. The software enabled marketing and sales organizations to catalogue their best practices and deliver just-in-time knowledge and advice to salespeople during actual, specific selling situations.

With WisdomWare, a salesperson would simply click on the type of person they were calling on plus a few other parameters, and the system would generate a pre-call "cheat sheet." This cheat sheet contained potential needs and pains to investigate, questions to determine which of those needs and pains were important to the customer, how to intelligently discuss them in the context of the products and services that best met those needs and pains, topics to avoid, how to respond to likely objections, and how to lay traps for the competition.

My experience with WisdomWare was the best of times and the worst of times. Although we generated a lot of interest and had some early sales successes, we were unable to close new customers fast enough to attract the level of funding needed to take the company to the next level. As a result, I was forced to close the company down in December of 1999, just three months before the market bubble burst and the economy went into a tailspin.

After dissolving the company, licking my wounds, and making sure my people found jobs, I decided it was time to retire. I took up golf from a specialized cart for disabled golfers I helped design, and I was able to get my game into the high 80s. After several months, however, I realized I was flunking full retirement, so I started to consult with a few companies to keep my hand in the game and fill in some of the time between golf matches.

THE ENLIGHTENMENT

I also spent a lot of time reflecting on WisdomWare, trying to figure out what went wrong. Sure, we made some strategic and operational mistakes, and the underlying technology infrastructure of the Internet wasn't robust enough in the late 1990s to do things as elegantly as we wanted. But we also did a lot of things right. We generated a lot of market buzz and interest, and even won the "Most Innovative New Product" award at a few industry shows. So why couldn't we get enough market traction to take the company to the next level?

While it was alive, WisdomWare had given me the unique opportunity to delve into the marketing and sales operations of more than 100 B-to-B companies. These companies were using all kinds of channel strategies to sell a wide range of products and services, including pharmaceutical and medical products, financial services, heavy industrial equipment, computers, enterprise software, and consulting. In going back over my experiences with these organizations, I was able to identify three issues at the core of WisdomWare's failure:

1. There wasn't enough pain in the marketplace in the late 1990s. Let's face it—selling in the 1990s was pretty easy. "C" players routinely made their quotas, and most marketing and sales organizations hit their numbers without worrying about alignment or effectiveness. While WisdomWare's prospects were excited and aroused by our product demos, and they all talked a good game about improving their execution, they weren't experiencing a whole lot of pain. As a result, they had little incentive to change their behavior. I should have picked up on this and understood the marketplace better early on, but in all honesty, I was blinded by our prospects' initial reaction to the "WisdomWare Vision." I didn't fully appreciate the impact the robust economy of the late 1990s really had on managers' attitudes and motivation until it was much too late.

2. Companies were way too product-focused. While almost every company was "talking the talk" about being customer-centric, in reality, few were really "walking the walk." Even though a lot of sales organizations were spending a fortune on sales training for solutions and consultative selling methodologies, most of this training was not producing the desired results because it was managed as a one-time event and rarely reinforced by day-to-day processes. To compound this, most marketing organizations had not been part of the solutions-selling initiative and they were still operating from an "inside-out" perspective, creating way too much product-centric collateral, presentations, and sales tools.

   WisdomWare forced B-to-B marketing and sales organizations to actually start walking the solutions-selling walk, and it required them to become much more precise in documenting the specific business issues and pains their customers were facing. It also required marketing to create more value-centric and sales-ready content that described how customers actually used their products and services to solve particular problems. While most of the sales organizations bought into this concept in a big way, a lot of the marketing people we encountered weren't able to venture outside of their comfort zones or to do all of the extra thinking or work needed to create the kind of sales-ready content the solutions-centric sales process required. They were perfectly happy to continue creating more feature-focused content and concentrating on the esoteric branding and creative issues that were more fun to work on.

3. We fell into the gap! The third issue was the tighter alignment and coordination that WisdomWare demanded between the marketing and sales

organizations. I made the mistake of falsely assuming that most B-to-B marketing and sales organizations had the ability to work pretty well together. As a result, one of the fundamental processes we built into WisdomWare was a collaborative value proposition and message development process to create what we called "Complete Value Propositions." This process included a closed-loop feedback system for salespeople to provide direct input to marketing, continuously improving and hardening the value propositions so they were more relevant and compelling to the marketplace.

It just seemed like common sense to me, but was I ever wrong! What we discovered in most companies was a culture where marketing and salespeople were so protective of their turf, they couldn't relate to each other on most issues. In fact, some of the marketing people we talked to even objected to WisdomWare's feedback system because they felt it would create more work for them and might increase complaints from salespeople. I found out later that some of these marketing people actually tried to sabotage our selling efforts.

These three revelations got my juices flowing, and the more people I talked to, the more it became apparent that the combination of a lack of customer focus and the marketing and sales disconnect had become a significant and pervasive problem that needed attention now. So I decided to write this book, and began talking about marketing and sales alignment with anybody who would listen to me.

What I quickly concluded from these discussions was that most marketing and sales executives react in much the same way I had before I started focusing on the disconnect. They significantly underestimate the cumulative amount of waste, cost, and lost opportunities caused by misalignment. As such, they rarely give the marketing and sales disconnect much concentrated thought, try to apply quick fixes, and treat the situation like the natural state of things, much like parents treat puberty. "Sure it's uncomfortable and unproductive, but there's not much we can do about it. Right?"

Wrong! In *Escaping the Black Hole,* I have tried to synthesize and clarify the issues that really drive the marketing and sales disconnect so the problem can be attacked in a rational and systematic fashion. To help managers accomplish this, I have developed two simple process models that align marketing and sales organizations around customers' needs and the way they buy things. These models are based upon two fundamental truths that jumped out at me the more I saw how companies were struggling with a dysfunctional relationship between their marketing and sales organizations:

1. In order to effectively sell solutions, marketing and sales organizations must institutionalize a more detailed understanding of the customer's business needs and the different implications of those needs on the individual stakeholders they market and sell to.

2. The way a company markets and sells must be subservient to the way their customers buy.

Because of their simplicity, these two process models can be implemented by companies of all sizes and stages of development. They combine the best new ideas and practices I uncovered during my research with some of the proven strategic and quality-management principles from well-accepted strategies, such as the Balanced Scorecard and Six Sigma.

THE SYNCHRONIZED MARKETING AND SALES ECOSYSTEM

By adopting some of the best practices contained in these new models, marketing and sales organizations will be able to operate more in concert than they ever have, creating a "Synchronized Marketing and Sales Ecosystem," where marketing and sales professionals become more coordinated and customer-focused, waste is eliminated, costs are controlled, and the execution of the fundamentals is continuously improved through:

- An integrated marketing and selling process that is tightly aligned with the specific buying practices of the marketplace. This buyer-centric marketing and selling model will tie the day-to-day marketing activities more closely to revenue, and help the marketing organizations become a vital and indispensable partner with sales.

- An integrated communications and knowledge-transfer process that's built around a revolutionary new best practice called Value Mapping™. Value Mapping is a reengineered version of the collaborative process I developed at WisdomWare, enabling companies to develop more Complete Value Propositions. The result is an integrated message mapping and sales coaching process that helps marketing and sales professionals actually map the DNA of their value propositions so they understand them better, institutionalize a more customer-centric culture, and embrace the principles of solution-centric selling.

While signs indicate the B-to-B economy is improving, most of us may never again see the kind of growth in business investment experienced during the 1990s. The only strategy that makes sense is to aggressively align marketing and sales organizations around what the customer really values, as well as the way they buy things. By doing this you will systematically improve the quality, execution, and impact of the materials marketing and sales professionals create and the activities they perform on a daily basis.

Minimizing misalignment is a never-ending journey. With some luck, this book will give you a few new ideas, stimulate some rigorous internal discussions, and provide the impetus for some of you to start transforming your marketing and sales organizations so that both can become more agile, interconnected, and effective.

To help you accomplish this, I have organized the rest of this book as follows:

1. Part I reviews the key findings of my research and identifies how certain market dynamics have collided with increasing misalignment to create the B-to-B Black Hole.

2. Part II introduces the two new process models that will minimize the impact of the B-to-B Black Hole and help create a Synchronized Marketing and Sales Ecosystem, where marketing and sales are more aligned around the customer.

3. Parts III and IV contain detailed roadmaps for implementing these process models and their best practices.

4. The Conclusion discusses how the dysfunction between marketing and sales presents an extraordinary opportunity for marketing executives, and the specific steps they can take to help their companies escape the damaging effects of the B-to-B Black Hole.

Good luck on your journey!

About the Author

Bob Schmonsees is a pioneer in customer relationship management (CRM) and knowledge management and a nationally recognized marketing and sales executive with over 35 years of experience building and running successful high-tech organizations. He has led sales and marketing in successful start-ups as well as large publicly traded software and services firms.

Bob has been featured in several national periodicals, including the *Wall Street Journal*, *Selling Power*, *ComputerWorld*, and *Knowledge Management*. Bob's company, R. J. Schmonsees & Associates, specializes in working with companies that require immediate and substantive improvements in their strategy, positioning, or their processes. R. J. Schmonsees & Associates can be found on the Internet at http://www.web2one.com/.

PART I

DISCOVERING THE EVENT HORIZON

"There has long been a critical, crippling disconnect between the marketing and sales functions in many business-to-business firms. This Marketing/Sales divide in B-to-B firms leads to a tremendous waste of marketing and sales effort and expenditures, inconsistent customer messaging, poor or delayed sales readiness, fewer sales calls as a result of protracted sales preparation time, and less effective selling dialogues. The bottom line: higher costs, lower revenues, and shrinking margins in an economy where these problems can put a firm out of business."

—ABERDEEN GROUP[1]

---

[1]"Bridging the Great Divide: Process, Technology, and the Marketing/Sales Interface," research published by Aberdeen Group (Wellesley, Massachusetts: 2002).

CHAPTER 1

The Schwarzschild Radius

IN 1916, A FEW MONTHS after Einstein announced his theories on relativity and gravity, the German astronomer and physicist Karl Schwarzschild published a paper describing a discrete, invisible perimeter surrounding the nucleus of a black hole in space. Often called the "Schwarzschild Radius," this perimeter has such a great gravitational force that the space/time continuum begins to warp. As a result, all matter, light, and energy passing this perimeter is sucked into an infinitely dense state called "singularity," never to be seen or heard from again. Schwarzschild called this point of no return "The Event Horizon," as shown in Figure 1.1.[2]

In summary, Schwarzschild concluded that black holes in space are larger than most people thought, and because of the density of singularity, no information can ever escape.

I can see some parallels between Schwarzschild's model and the disconnect between marketing and sales organizations. As I mentioned in the Introduction, from late 2000 through the middle of 2004, I read more than 150 articles, studies, and white papers, and conducted hundreds of interviews on marketing and sales alignment and effectiveness. These included detailed discussions with the executives from B-to-B companies of various sizes, industry analysts, Customer Relationship Management (CRM) vendors, sales training companies, and marketing and sales consultants.

What I discovered from this process was that the B-to-B marketing and sales model was broken in a lot of companies and had been slowly breaking down for a couple of decades due to the confluence of two key factors:

1. The rapid change and increasing amount of both natural and artificially induced complexity that all B-to-B companies have to deal with in terms of market dynamics, products, distribution channels, and communications

---

[2]"About Schwarzschild Geometry," http://casa.colorado.edu/~ajsh/schwp.html, November, 2004.

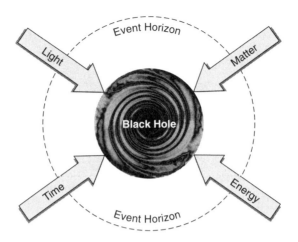

FIGURE 1.1 *THE EVENT HORIZON*

technologies. This requires more customer focus, better messaging, more informed sales channels, and improved execution of the marketing and selling fundamentals.

2. An increasing amount of marketing and sales misalignment in almost every company I talked to. Unfortunately, there will always be some natural tension and disconnects between marketing and sales professionals. But I found the gap between a lot of marketing and sales organizations was actually growing wider. This widening reduced the quality of execution, and it injected a lot of waste and inefficiencies into the go-to-market model.

THE B-TO-B BLACK HOLE

This confluence between the increasing complexity and hyper-change with the decreasing marketing and sales alignment has created a phenomenon I call the B-to-B Black Hole. It's where a lot of costs, time, and resources are wasted, and viable marketing and sales opportunities are missed and lost forever. Almost every executive I talked to during my research admits to this waste and inefficiency at some level, but as I mentioned in the Introduction, the fact that misalignment seems like "the natural state of things" leads many of them to conclude there's not much they can do about it, so they might as well just grin and bear it.

I also discovered through my research that the symptoms of misalignment are often so pervasive and manifest themselves in so many different places that it is extremely difficult for most executives to perceive and calibrate the actual amount of waste and dysfunction and fully appreciate the extent of the problem. As a result, almost all of them underestimate the total impact of misalignment and the size and scope of the B-to-B Black Hole, just like the physicists did before Schwarzschild published his theories. As the following statistics show, this problem has now become a significant factor in the overall marketing and sales productivity equation:

- 25 percent of all marketing and sales resources are routinely wasted.[3]
- 70 to 80 percent of leads generated by marketing are never followed up.[4]
- Only 29 percent of a salesperson's time is actually spent selling.[5]
- 80 percent of sales support experts are regularly used inappropriately.[6]

The robust economy and seller's market of the 1990s also helped create a condition similar to the state of singularity described by Schwarzschild, in which the information on what was happening deep inside the B-to-B Black Hole never saw the light of day. This, along with the fact that it is human nature to ignore threats until they become a crisis, helped mask the rapid growth of the problem (see Figure 1.2). As a result, many of these symptoms went undetected and unaddressed as companies continued to make their numbers. When the economy faltered in 2000, however, execution of the marketing and sales fundamentals became critical, and the depth and magnitude of the B-to-B Black Hole was exposed for all to see.

All at once, the dysfunctional relationship between marketing and sales organizations became evident, and CEOs and boards of directors started shooting their marketing and sales executives in an attempt to find a "quick fix" to the problem. Of course, there is no quick fix. Minimizing the damage of the B-to-B Black Hole demands that management attack the root causes of the marketing and sales disconnect and implement processes that drive

---

[3]Study of 200 product managers, conducted by Pragmatic Marketing (2002).

[4]Sheryl Kingstone, "Improving Sales Effectiveness in a Down Economy," published by Yankee Group (Boston, Massachusetts: 2002): 10.

[5]"Hesitate Before You Automate," *The Culpepper Letter,* published by Fenemore Group (July, 1997).

[6]Study of 200 product managers, conducted by Pragmatic Marketing (2002).

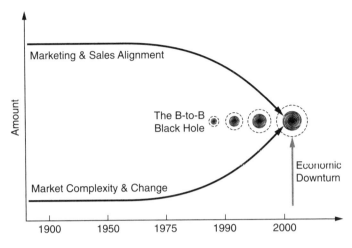

FIGURE 1.2 *THE GROWTH OF THE B-TO-B BLACK HOLE*

organizational and cultural transformation. This requires a better under-standing of where you are, how you got there, and what's really going on under the surface.

THE FRONT HALF OF THE FUNNEL

As I talked to more people and began to study this phenomenon in more detail so I could synthesize the problem, it became obvious that the B-to-B Black Hole has its own Event Horizon where the damage from the marketing and sales disconnect is the greatest. Figure 1.3 illustrates how this point of no return occurs during the early stages of the marketing and sales process, when marketing and sales professionals are generating demand, developing the needs of their prospects and customers, and qualifying those opportuni-ties. The front half of the marketing and sales funnel is where most of the waste and inefficiencies occur and where the disconnect between the two organizations has the most negative impact on the enterprise.

There are several reasons why increasing amounts of costs, time, and resources are consumed during the early stages of the marketing and selling process:

- There are fewer opportunities today due to the economic climate, so demand is harder to generate and high-quality leads are harder to uncover.

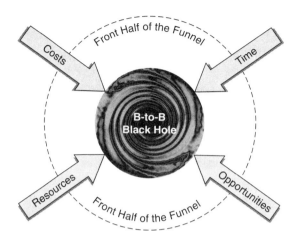

FIGURE 1.3 *THE B-TO-B BLACK HOLE*

- Increasing complexity and changing market dynamics have made the needs development and qualification process much more difficult, and it is no longer just about determining whether or not the customer has the budget. In fact, in a lot of cases there is no budget, and vendors can no longer wait until their prospects have money on the table before engaging them in a substantive manner.

- Defining needs and qualifying prospects often involves multiple meetings with multiple constituencies and individuals, each having their own scheduling requirements. What's worse is that many of these people may be in different locations and different time zones. Not only does the actual increase in meetings impact the time and resources that are expended during the front half of the funnel, but the logistical challenge of getting people in the same place at the same time for a face-to-face presentation grows almost exponentially as more people on the prospect's side become involved in the buying process.

- However, I have come to believe that it is the misalignment between marketing and sales assets, activities, and processes that may well be the most important contributor to the Event Horizon of the B-to-B Black Hole. That is what the rest of this book is all about.

As Figure 1.4 indicates, the four factors on the left side of the funnel have had a debilitating effect on productivity and effectiveness during the most crucial time of the marketing and sales process.

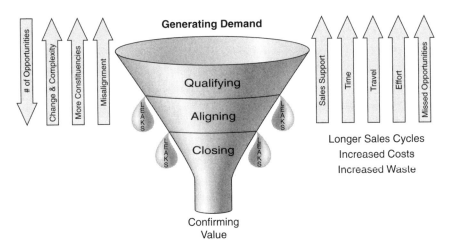

FIGURE 1.4 THE FRONT HALF OF THE FUNNEL

These factors have significantly increased the negative impacts of the B-to-B Black Hole, specifically:

- Sales cycles lengthen because of the increased number of meetings, scheduling delays, and no-shows that invariably happen when multiple people are involved.
- Sales costs, especially sales support and travel costs, increase.
- Sales support resources are wasted when salespeople don't qualify effectively. As a result, some of these valuable experts become frustrated and disenchanted.
- Some good opportunities are missed because valuable resources are consumed while sales people chase unqualified ones.

WE HAVE SEEN THE ENEMY AND IT IS US!

As I began to pick a lot of smart people's brains on this issue and started to look at the gap between marketing and sales through a microscope, I discovered that much of the growth in the B-to-B Black Hole was, in fact, self-inflicted. While there was little management could do about the economy or market complexity, it became evident that there were several strategic and operational mistakes made by many marketing and sales executives during the last twenty years that actually widened the gap between marketing and sales. As I mentioned in the Introduction, I made most of these same mistakes myself over the years, and many more than once.

1. Failing to understand the true nature of marketing and sales. First and foremost, at its core, the B-to-B marketing and sales process is one of continuous learning, facilitated through the sharing of information and the transferring of knowledge between marketing, sales, partners, prospects, and customers. When management views marketing and sales as a knowledge-transfer function, it becomes clear that improving the quality of the knowledge-transfer experience translates into a greater ability to influence people's perceptions, attitudes, and behavior, which is the obvious ultimate objective.

2. Failing to embrace processes and quality management principles. Integrated processes are the key to increasing alignment and continuously improving the execution of the fundamentals, but unfortunately, even with the massive investments that companies made implementing Customer Relationship Management (CRM) systems:

   - 58 percent of companies have never formally defined the steps of their selling process.[7]

   - 80 percent of those that have defined their sales process have not implemented an effective pipeline management process.

   - 75 percent do not have a systematic process for managing leads.

3. Failing to institutionalize customer-centric cultures. During the last decade, people talked a great deal about focusing on the customer, and a lot of companies implemented CRM systems to gather more accurate customer transaction information so they could improve customer service. This has worked to a point. CRM systems have made service organizations more responsive and customer-focused but, as we will see later, service is just one of the dimensions of implementing a truly customer-centric culture. The hard reality is that most companies have yet to crack the code for making their marketing and sales organizations truly customer-centric.

   For example, my research indicates that more than 90 percent of those companies who had defined their selling process in their CRM system have not aligned that process with the way their customers were actually buying things. Additionally, even though billions have been spent on solutions-centric selling methodologies and training, most marketing

---

[7]Barry Trailer and Jim Dickie, "Sales Effectiveness Report," published by CSO Insights (2004): 2.

and sales organizations do not embrace the fundamental principles of these methodologies in their day-to-day activities. More importantly, most B-to-B companies have failed to institutionalize both an in-depth understanding of the specific business issues and problems that their prospects were trying to solve, and how their customers actually used their solutions to solve those problems and create value. As a result:

- Most companies continue to go to market with an inside-out perspective, and there is still too much focus on products and features.
- 75 percent of solutions-selling initiatives have failed to generate any ROI.[8]
- 65 percent of companies are spending more on pre-sales support than they had previously.
- 75 percent of marketing and salespeople are unable to consistently and effectively articulate their value propositions.[9]
- 80 percent of companies do not deliver targeted messages to different audiences, constituencies, and stakeholders.[10]

4. Failing to aggressively and systematically manage intellectual assets. Outside of the people, the intellectual assets that support the value propositions are some of an enterprise's most important marketing and sales assets. Nevertheless, effective processes for organizing and managing the raw marketing and sales knowledge, as well as the sanctioned content, have often been an afterthought. In fact, my research indicates that more than 60 percent of B-to-B companies do not have a systematic process for managing and continually improving marketing and sales content, and 85 percent of them do not have a formalized process for sharing competitive and market intelligence or best sales practices. And, when these assets are managed, it's usually delegated to the IT department and the Webmaster, who typically approach the problem like a librarian. Thus, more than 75 percent of marketing executives believe they are doing a poor job of managing marketing and sales messages and content.[11]

---

[8]Chandru Krishnamurthy, Juliet Johansson, and Hank Schlissberg, "Marketing Solutions," McKinsey & Co. (Atlanta: 2003).

[9]Marketing Alignment Benchmark Study, conducted by Holden Corporation (Hoffman Estates, Illinois: 2001): 2.

[10]Bill Glazier, "Making Marketing Messaging Meaningful," published by the CMO Council (Palo Alto, California: June 3, 2004): 2.

[11]Bill Glazier, "Making Marketing Messaging Meaningful," published by the CMO Council (Palo Alto, California: June 3, 2004): 2.

When you consider both the visible and invisible costs of developing and leveraging these assets, this lack of a systematic approach to managing the marketing and sales knowledge and content that supports the value proposition messages has an enormous impact on productivity. As we will see later in this book, it significantly increases the total cost of marketing and sales, as well as the size and impact of the B-to-B Black Hole. For example:

- 80 to 90 percent of marketing collateral is considered useless by sales.[12]
- Salespeople spend typically 30 to 50 hours per month searching for information and re-creating customer-facing content.[13]
- 80 to 90 percent of the customer-facing content created by salespeople is inaccurate and dilutes the brand.[14]

My research has convinced me that the gravitational pull on time and resources from this Event Horizon will only get more powerful as some new market dynamics and communication models become day-to-day realities. This means prudent marketing and sales executives need to start addressing marketing and sales misalignment now before the B-to-B Black Hole consumes their organizations.

During the next several chapters, I will discuss the increasing complexity and changing market dynamics that demand increased marketing and sales alignment, more integrated processes, and a true customer-centric culture. I will also go into more detail on the strategic and operational management mistakes that have widened the gap between marketing and sales organizations over the last two decades and increased both the size and impact of the B-to-B Black Hole.

---

[12]Proceedings of the Customer Message Management Forums, published by the American Marketing Association and Ventaso (2002 and 2003).

[13]"Bridging the Great Divide: Process, Technology, and the Marketing/Sales Interface," research published by Aberdeen Group (Wellesley, Massachusetts: 2002).

[14]Proceedings of the Customer Message Management Forums, published by the American Marketing Association and Ventaso (2002 and 2003).

CHAPTER 2

The Increasing Market Complexity

THE B-TO-B MARKETING and sales environment is a complex and often chaotic environment to begin with, and there are many factors that contribute to this complexity. I contend, however, that the most significant of these factors is the fact that the B-to-B marketing and selling process involves teams selling to teams. There are marketing teams, selling teams, and buying teams containing people with different roles, responsibilities, and constantly changing objectives, both business and personal.

The fundamental nature of teams in itself demands a high degree of marketing and sales coordination and alignment. But on top of this, five inter-related factors have made things much more complex over the last few decades. They have made a company's value propositions more difficult to create, hone, and deliver, and this has put a lot of additional pressure on the efficiency and execution of the marketing and sales process. The end result is that these five factors demand a much higher degree of marketing and sales integration and alignment in order to minimize the effects of the B-to-B Black Hole. These five factors are:

1. The complexity of customer business problems
2. The number of stakeholders who participate in the buying process
3. The complexity of the buying process
4. The complexity of solutions
5. The complexity of the distribution model

THE INCREASING COMPLEXITY
OF BUSINESS PROBLEMS

Over the last decade, the combination of the rapid advances in computer and communications technologies, increasing globalization, and heightened competition has rapidly increased the complexity of almost all of the issues and problems that business executives have to deal with. Today, the specifics of a particular business problem often differ by industry segment and even between companies in the same industry, depending on factors such as location, market position, culture, organization, technology infrastructure, and business model. All of this increased complexity impacts the marketing and sales activities that occur during the early stages of the funnel.

THE GROWING NUMBER OF STAKEHOLDERS

In addition to complex business problems, the solution-oriented B-to-B sale almost always involves dealing with multiple constituencies and stakeholders. Unfortunately, as the complexity of business problems has increased, the number of potential stakeholders involved in the buying process also has grown at a significant rate. In fact, in 2004, Sirius Decisions reported that over the last several years an average of 3.5 more people have become involved in the typical enterprise buying decision.[1]

A lot of these additional stakeholders bring different issues, objectives, and needs of their own to the table that have to be addressed before a sale is actually made. They can also have different perceptions regarding the same business issue, depending on where they are in the organization and their own individual objectives, interests, and political status. This brings us to what I call "The Cascading Need Phenomenon," illustrated in Figure 2.1, which is one of the most challenging issues faced by B-to-B marketing and selling organizations because it increases both the number and the complexity of a company's value propositions exponentially.

In most sales opportunities, what begins as a single business problem can quickly turn into a whole collection of different symptoms, objectives, and pains. As Figure 2.1 shows, a B-to-B salesperson, regardless of the primary decision maker for his or her product or service, may ultimately have to address a complex hierarchy of stakeholders and unique business needs both above and below that primary decision maker. For example:

1. The CEO has the strategic need to increase profits.
2. This, in turn, generates multiple sub-needs of various types, such as the need for the marketing VP to cut costs or the sales VP to increase revenues.

---

[1]Sirius Decisions Perspectives News Letter, http://www.siriusdecisions.com, May 10, 2004.

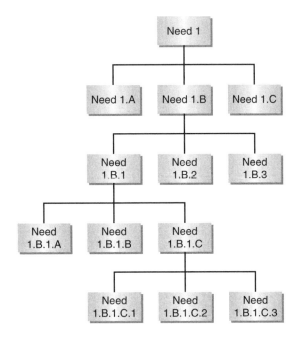

FIGURE 2.1 *THE CASCADING NEED PHENOMENON*

3. Each of these sub-needs generates more needs at lower levels in the organization. In the case of increasing sales, for example, the sales operations manager may now have a need to improve the quality of sales training. And so it goes.

4. Each stakeholder on the buying team, whether a decision maker or an influencer, has different requirements for content and information.

5. Finally, most complex sales traverse multiple need hierarchies because today's products and services often have implications for other parts of the buying organization that may have conflicting objectives and pains. For example, in this scenario, the sales operations manager's training need may also have significant resource implications for the product marketing organization.

As companies flatten their management structures and implement more matrix-based and networked organizational structures, more stakeholders will likely be brought into the buying process. And with each new stakeholder, the complexity of the selling and buying process has the potential to expand significantly, adversely threatening and delaying the sales event.

The Cascading Need Phenomenon has significant ramifications on how marketing and sales organizations develop, manage, and communicate the many different value propositions provided by their solutions to different stakeholders. It requires that both organizations embrace the principles of solution-centric selling so they gain and institutionalize a more detailed understanding of the specific needs of those different stakeholders. It also means that the traditional one-size-fits-all approach to marketing communications, sales collateral, and selling tools just won't cut it. This is a thorny problem, and few companies have cracked the code. In fact, more than 75 percent of the companies surveyed in a 2004 study by the CMO Council said they did not have an effective messaging platform to address the information needs of multiple constituencies and stakeholders.[2]

The Cascading Need Phenomenon is the primary reason successful salespeople cultivate someone in the buying organization who becomes their "Internal Champion." In many sales situations, most of the actual selling and buying conversations happen without a salesperson present to promote and defend the value of their solution. Accordingly, the Internal Champions must be able to effectively carry the many different value proposition messages forward to the various stakeholders. This "carry forward" process requires marketing and sales organizations to quickly and efficiently transfer enough knowledge to their Internal Champions. These people need simple, yet effective, selling tools to help them explain and validate the different value propositions and to address the concerns of their fellow employees after the salesperson has left the building. Most companies, however, have not developed the kinds of selling tools their Internal Champions need to adequately champion their solutions.

THE COMPLEXITY OF THE BUYING PROCESS

Companies typically go through a repeatable set of steps when they purchase complex products and services. And while there are lots of ways to describe this buying process, I have found it productive to view it as six steps within two main phases—a pre-commitment phase and a post-commitment phase.

---

[2] Bill Glazier, "Making Marketing Messaging Meaningful," published by the CMO Council (Palo Alto, California: June 3, 2004): 2.

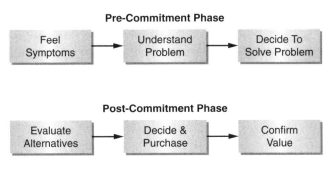

FIGURE 2.2 *THE B-TO-B BUYING PROCESS*

In my research for this book, I was surprised to discover that more than 90 percent of the companies I talked to that had implemented a structured sales process in their CRM system had never taken the time to identify and formally document the specific steps of their customers' buying processes so they could align the two together. The few that had, however, were able to get their marketing and sales organizations to visualize their role as eliminating the friction between the different phases of the buying process and helping their prospects and customers complete that process as quickly and efficiently as possible. As we will discuss in later chapters, this detailed understanding of the customer's buying process, and the distinction between selling prospects something and helping them buy, has a significant impact on marketing and sales strategy, tactics, and deliverables.

Of course, the B-to-B buying process is never quite this simple, and the increasing complexity of business problems, plus the growing number of stakeholders, only compounds the complexity. We can assume that:

- Individual stakeholders in the customer organization will be on different steps at any one point in time.
- Stakeholders will jump back and forth between steps throughout the buying process.
- The information and content needs differ depending on the stakeholder and the step.
- A stakeholder can effectively absorb information only in the context of the step he or she is actually on.

- Understanding which step the stakeholder is actually on, no matter what the stakeholder tells you, is critical to the success of any sales or marketing communication.
- Most stakeholders will adjust their vision of the ideal solution several times throughout the buying process.

Each of these factors increases the need for crisper and more stakeholder-focused value propositions, higher-quality content, and improved integration and execution of the branding strategy, the lead generation programs, and the selling activities.

As we entered the twenty-first century, money became tighter and discretionary spending was virtually eliminated, which has also complicated the buying process. The hard reality of the new economy is that prospects—to re-interpret an old Carly Simon lyric—"only have time for the pain," and buy few, if any, products or services merely to increase convenience or slightly improve something that's already working. With all of the issues facing management today, they only make major purchases or change things when:

1. They are in a great deal of pain, and perceive the pain is going to get worse.
2. The executive team is personally embarrassed.
3. The executive team is in political jeopardy because they are not taking visible action to alleviate the pain.

The end result is that there are a lot more activities to perform and questions to answer before a company feels it has enough information about its problems to make a commitment to solve them.

During the seller's market of the 1990s, most marketing and sales organizations focused either on eliminating prospects from consideration if they didn't have a budget or on pushing qualified prospects through the closing process. This was done at the expense of a focus on needs development, so today, few salespeople possess this fundamental and critical skill. This is one of the major contributing factors to the waste and inefficiencies driving the size of the Event Horizon at the front half of the funnel.

In the future, marketing and sales will need to shift their emphasis to the pre-commitment phase. They will be spending more time and energy in the front half of the funnel, so they will need to become much more effective in the execution of lead generation and needs development activities. As such, both marketing and sales professionals need to better understand customers' and stakeholders' business needs, and embrace and institutionalize the principles of solution-centric selling. This will enable them to become more adept at identifying and fully understanding the customer's issues and pains, and to do a much better job of mapping those pains to the specific capabilities of their products and services through their collateral, selling tools, and other communications activities.

Finally, one of the hard realities of the new economy is that deals can be lost even after they are closed. This means more sales attention and support resources need to be applied after the sale has been made to continuously confirm that the customer is getting the value they expect.

THE COMPLEXITY OF THE SOLUTIONS

In order to address the increasing complexity of business problems and the growing number of stakeholder needs, the product and service offerings of most B-to-B companies, as well as their competition, deliver value in more ways and get more complex every day. This ever-changing competitive landscape requires a more systematic and coordinated way for sales and marketing organizations to share best sales practices and competitive intelligence. Yet, most companies have not figured out how to solve this problem either.

Another factor that increases product complexity is the fact that information technology is becoming an integral part of many traditional business products and services. A FedEx salesperson, for example, now has more than 200 different service offerings they need to master, many of which contain an information or communications technology component.[3] I believe that most B-to-B companies can now be viewed as a technology company in some fashion or another. As a result, many of the buying patterns of the Technology Adoption Life Cycle described by Geoffrey Moore in his landmark book, *Crossing The Chasm,* now apply to the selling process, increasing the amount of business products and services that on the surface would not normally be classified as technology products.[4]

---

[3]Andres Davis, Federal Express Corp., report from the Third CMM Forum, November, 2002.
[4]Geoffrey A. Moore, *Crossing the Chasm,* Harper Business, 1991.

The rapid increase in product complexity has also had a major impact on the way companies differentiate themselves. Emphasizing feature-level differentiation used to be an important positioning strategy for many B-to-B companies. Today, this is rarely the case because:

- Increased product complexity has made substantive differentiation more difficult to create, identify, and explain.
- Most of today's products are so feature rich that most customers will never even use some of these differentiated features.
- Product development cycles are so short that feature differentiation does not last very long.
- Most buying decisions are now being made at higher levels in the organization where feature differentiation is not that important.

This lack of product differentiation increases the importance of business practices and business models as key components of a company's overall value proposition. These messages are directed at a higher-level audience, and they require a different strategy for marketing content and selling tools.

COMPLEXITY OF THE DISTRIBUTION MODEL

Globalization combined with rapidly changing market dynamics has required many companies to develop complex distribution strategies with multiple channels. This increasing amount of alliances and re-sellers has increased the complexity of the selling team, as well as the complexity of the information needed by both the supplier of the product or service and the channel partner. In fact, in many cases where there is a complex enterprise solution required, the selling team includes people from multiple vendors. The end result is a double whammy. Both the selling and buying teams have become larger and more complex, requiring improved coordination and a more integrated and synchronized marketing and sales process. Selling tools also need to reflect the different needs of a multi-tiered distribution model. These new tools have to help partners become better at executing the activities during the front half of the funnel.

THE IMPACT ON THE MESSAGES

The increasing complexity of business problems, stakeholder needs, and solutions has significantly increased the complexity of the average value proposition. Today's B-to-B solutions deliver value in a lot of different ways to a lot of different people creating a lot of different value propositions.

However, my research indicates that most companies only focus on a single or a small subset of these value propositions and the knowledge underlying the others is rarely, if ever, managed in a systematic fashion. And even though many of these other value proposition messages are some of the most important intellectual assets of an enterprise, in most companies, nobody actually owns them. In the past, marketing organizations used to own the value proposition messages when they were simpler and more generic, but over the last couple of decades many marketing organizations have abdicated that responsibility to sales because it just became too onerous.

More than 90 percent of the companies I talked to for this book had no process to document the myriad ways they deliver value to different constituencies in a systematic fashion. These nuggets of knowledge were usually scattered throughout the enterprise in documents, e-mails, and in the minds of their subject matter experts. This has led to a lack of clear, consistent messages at best, and at worst confusion.

It is this lack of a formal message management process that extends the ramp-up times for salespeople and increases the size and impact of the B-to-B Black Hole. I contend that unless this situation is addressed in a systematic fashion, it will only continue to get worse.

CHAPTER 3

The Changing Market Dynamics

IN ADDITION TO THE increasing complexity in the B-to-B go-to-market model, there are three new market dynamics that, when taken together, fundamentally change the marketing and sales game forever. Some of these trends have been building for a long time, but when combined with the tougher economic realities of the twenty-first century, their potential impact on marketing and sales effectiveness and the size of the B-to-B Black Hole is considerable. These new market dynamics are:

1. The integration of services with products
2. The power shift to the buyer
3. Shrinking message shelf lives

INTEGRATING SERVICES WITH PRODUCTS

An increasing amount of services are now being bundled with many B-to-B products, and these are often coupled with customization and systems integration as part of an enterprise solution or industrial purchase. This means that many of the elements making up a company's value propositions are becoming less tangible. As Tom Peters says in *Re-imagine!*, "Welcome to a world where value (damn near all value) is based on intangibles—not lumpy objects, but weightless figments of the Economic Imagination."[1]

These less tangible value propositions require a lot more alignment between marketing and sales organizations. They need to be backed up with more specific marketing content and better quality selling tools in order to provide demonstrable and measurable validation of the actual value. As Josh Rossman, who runs Cisco's marketing and sales effectiveness initiative, told me in a personal interview, "Our customers are far more demanding of

---

[1]Tom Peters, *Re-Imagine! Business Excellence in a Disruptive Age* (New York: DK Publishing, 2003).

value information for our services than they are for our products. That's why we aggressively document our references, and why we built a comprehensive ROI calculator for our support services. Without tools like these, it's difficult for our salespeople to explain and our customers to fully appreciate the real value of our total solution."

Complete, compelling, and precise value propositions are more important than ever. As services become more and more intertwined with products, pricing and especially discounting become critical. I have worked with several companies that were integrating an increasing amount of services into their solutions, and it is a challenge for both the salespeople and the buyers to understand the difference between discounting products and services.

The key difference is that discounts negotiated on a product have little, if any, direct effect on the deliverable because the product, in most cases, has already been built and the manufacturing costs are already sunk. As a result, any discount goes right into the buyer's pocket and quality is not affected. Discounting services, however, is a different ball game. Discounts are granted before the service is manufactured, and they directly impact how much the vendor can spend on delivery. As the government has found out through the low-bid process, this often impacts quality, increases risks, and can drive up the total cost over the long run.

Additionally, as B-to-B solutions contain an ever-increasing amount of value-added services, the time, cost, and effort associated with shifting vendors are often reduced. This ease of movement requires marketing and sales organizations to pay more attention than ever to confirming that the customer has actually received the value expected and feels satisfied. That's why many companies like Cisco have implemented formal post-sales assessment programs to validate and confirm the value of the total relationship with their customers.

THE BUYER/SELLER POWER SHIFT

During the last decade, there has also been a significant shift in power and control from the seller to the buyer of B-to-B products and services. Prospects have become indifferent to all but the most provocative sales pitches, and many of them won't return phone calls or read e-mails from salespeople. Although it would be easy to blame the current economic conditions for this ambivalence and power shift, and conclude that it's a

cyclical phenomenon, my research indicates this is part of a more fundamental restructuring of the buyer/seller relationship. This shift has been
brought about by the convergence of one economic and three non-
economic factors.

The economic factor is that budgets are rarely developed in the pre-
commitment phase of the buying process anymore, so companies have to
get used to spending marketing and sales resources without the promise
that the customer will ever buy anything. This places a premium on better
value messages and the selling tools created for developing needs and qualifying prospects, as well as on actually helping them get budgets approved.

The three non-economic factors are:

1. B-to-B buyers are better informed than they used to be, and the vendors
   have lost the "knowledge advantage" they once had over their prospects
   and customers. Before the mid-90s, salespeople often had more recent and
   more accurate information than their prospects and customers, and this
   knowledge became a source of power and control. Obviously, the Internet
   has changed this forever. Over the last five years, this knowledge advantage
   has been dissipated, and often reversed, as buyers at all levels of the customer's organization have 24-7 access to up-to-date information. Furthermore, prospects can now get information not only from the vendor's site
   but also from competitors, analysts, blogs, and chat rooms where the
   vendor has little, if any, control over the information.

2. Now that prospects and customers have gained the knowledge advantage,
   they have become insatiable for high-quality content and up-to-date,
   accurate information. Their higher expectations have raised the bar on
   vendors, and they now demand specific, relevant, and personalized
   answers quickly. They just won't tolerate salespeople who consume their
   time and deliver little extra value during the sales process.

   As T. Michael Glen, president of FedEx services, says in the book, *Inside
   the Minds of Leading Marketers,* "Customers will not tolerate information
   that's not useful for them. There will be more resistance to generic forms of
   communication. Customers will expect us to understand their requirements
   and to address them with relevant advertising, promotion, and collateral.
   Obviously, technology is going to drive this change in a significant way."[2]

---

[2]T. Michael Glen, *Inside the Minds of Leading Marketers* (Boston, Massachusetts: Aspatore
Books, 2001).

3. Finally, prospects and customers have become more sophisticated about the buying and selling process. Many of them have attended training on negotiation skills, and they have learned how to lay traps for salespeople and to counteract many sales techniques traditionally taught in sales training classes. Because of this increased sophistication, their expectations are higher, not only in terms of the products and services they buy, but also in terms of the way they are sold to.

As a result of this power shift, marketing and sales organizations must approach the marketplace with a more outside-in orientation. They not only need to understand the customer history from their CRM systems, but they also need a better understanding of the customer's business issues and pains and how their customers actually go about buying things. On top of this more complete understanding of the customer, salespeople also have to constantly find ways to add value above and beyond their company's products and services. They need to view themselves as educators and facilitators, not just closers. This means that marketing organizations need to create selling tools that help their salespeople and partners have more intelligent business conversations with their customers and bring additional perceptible value to the table so that they become a key part of the solution, and as such, the overall value proposition. This will require more collaboration and a significant mind shift for many marketing professionals.

SHRINKING MESSAGE SHELF LIVES

As David Weinberger says in the landmark book on the Internet, *The Cluetrain Manifesto*, "For every product, there are dozens or hundreds of facts . . . useful facts."[3] When linked together these facts, along with other ideas, insights, and chunks of information, create what I call a "Complete Value Proposition."

The bad news for B-to-B marketing and sales professionals is that rapid innovation combined with the increasing complexity of products and markets are changing the accuracy and currency of these different chunks of information at a faster rate than ever. As a recent Aberdeen report stated,

---

[3]Rick Levine, Christopher Locke, Doc Searls, and David Weinberger, *The Cluetrain Manifesto* (Cambridge, Massachusetts: Perseus Books, 1999).

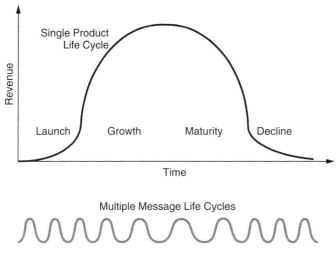

FIGURE 3.1 SHRINKING MESSAGE SHELF LIVES

"Product development and distribution cycles are accelerating faster than the marcom processes that create marketing content and product messaging materials."[4]

All this change has significantly reduced the shelf life of a lot of product-focused messages and the associated collateral. And this requires the positioning, value propositions, and Sanctioned Content produced by marketing to be constantly reviewed, refreshed, and refined. We are all familiar with the typical product life cycle, in which revenues follow a bell curve from product inception through market acceptance, product growth, and finally to product maturity and its corresponding phase of declining revenue. Today, however, as Figure 3.1 indicates, most product life cycles include multiple "message life cycles." When these frequent message life cycles are combined with the increased complexities discussed in the previous chapter, the velocity of message change is often overwhelming.

As soon as a message begins to work, something in the marketplace changes, or the competition adds a new feature, and marketing and sales organizations have to adjust. As you can see in Figure 3.1, the velocity of

---

[4]"Bridging the Great Divide: Process, Technology, and the Marketing/Sales Interface," research published by Aberdeen Group (Wellesley, Massachusetts: 2002).

product message change fluctuates with the stages of the product and market life cycle. During product launch and decline, for example, the messages are more fluid with shorter shelf lives. This is due to the fact that marketing and sales organizations are going through an aggressive learning curve during product rollout, and they are constantly trying new approaches during the declining revenue phase.

This shrinking message shelf life is exacerbated by the natural inclination to try to differentiate a product or service by how it is described. In B-to-B environments, the "new thing" is sometimes so desirable that marketing professionals often invent new ways, phrases, and acronyms to describe the "old thing" just to make it seem new. Nowhere is this phenomenon more pronounced than in the high-tech industry, where marketing professionals are constantly changing the acronyms and inventing new categories to create the façade of differentiation.

Dealing with these shorter message shelf lives has become increasingly cumbersome with the explosion in the total amount of the marketing-developed (as well as sales-developed) content that needs to be managed and kept consistent. The situation requires much more customer-centric messaging, increased alignment between marketing and sales professionals, and a more systematic approach to creating and managing the messages and the marketing and sales content.

Unfortunately, as I mentioned in the last chapter, what I have found is that most companies don't have a disciplined message management process and continue to develop messages in a fragmented and chaotic way, resulting in lots of inconsistencies and too much product-focus. As a result, marketing and sales become less connected because sales creates its own messaging, and the Sanctioned Content produced by marketing becomes less and less relevant to salespeople. Ultimately, the marketing and sales relationship grows more dysfunctional, and the B-to-B Black Hole gets bigger and bigger.

CHAPTER 4

The Changing Communications Model

PRIOR TO THE 1980S, B-to-B marketing organizations rarely communicated directly with prospects and customers. When they did, it was primarily through broadcast medium like print advertising, where information was very general and flowed only in one direction. Marketing and sales collateral was delivered directly to the sales organization, who controlled what customers and prospects ultimately received. Finally, telephones were used primarily to set up face-to-face meetings, not to conduct substantive selling and sales support activities.

Between 1980 and 2000 however, the B-to-B marketing and sales content and communication model was fundamentally altered due to five major factors:

1. The emergence of telesales as a viable selling technique for B-to-B products. It wasn't that long ago that the concept of telephone-based selling was considered a radical departure for B-to-B sales organizations. I can remember in 1984, I thought a friend of mine (who is now worth several hundred million) was nuts when he started a company to sell a $7,500 software system over the phone. But once companies saw the cost and time benefits of telephone-based selling, salespeople were trained in these techniques, and new telephone technologies, such as voice mail and phone conferencing, were developed and quickly embraced by sales organizations. As a result, telesales has evolved into an important component of the B-to-B sales model. Now companies routinely sell complex products and services priced at more than $100,000 without ever making a face-to-face sales call.

2. The emergence of direct mail as a major marketing channel. Direct mail blossomed as a demand generation strategy, and this gave B-to-B marketing professionals an opportunity to bypass the sales channels and go directly to the marketplace with an unfiltered message and content they thought appropriate. By the early 1990s, prospects who requested

information often received large "fulfillment kits" with as many brochures and press releases as the folder could hold, long before the salesperson made contact. Salespeople were no longer the primary filter for the information prospects and customers received.

3. The emergence of computer-based content development tools. The emergence of products such as Microsoft Word® and PowerPoint® enabled sales and sales support people to modify sanctioned marketing material and create their own customer-facing content.

4. The emergence of e-mail as a broad-based communication tool. Employees have been using internal e-mail systems on IBM mainframes to communicate with each other since the late 1970s. But once the Internet extended e-mail beyond the enterprise, it quickly developed into the primary text-based communication vehicle for salespeople, as well as a major broadcast medium for marketing organizations to generate leads and extend their direct contact with the marketplace.

5. The emergence of the Web as the primary delivery vehicle for customer-facing content. By the late 1990s, both B-to-B marketing and sales organizations were using the Web to deliver all kinds of content and collateral directly to prospects and customers at all stages of the marketing and sales funnel. This joint delivery paradigm inevitably required tighter alignment, coordination, and collaboration between marketing and sales organizations.

During the first few years of the twenty-first century, however, there have been three inter-related communication and technology developments that will fundamentally alter the B-to-B communication environment forever. These developments will require a much greater level of alignment and coordination between marketing and sales organizations. These three trends are:

1. The explosive growth in rich media, especially PowerPoint
2. The ability to dynamically generate content
3. The growth in collaborative technologies

THE EXPLOSIVE GROWTH IN POWERPOINT

Richer media has become prevalent in everything from proposals to e-mails, and the use of PowerPoint has been growing for over a decade. This growth, however, has increased exponentially during the last several years, and in many B-to-B companies PowerPoint has now become the primary method for both internal and external communications.

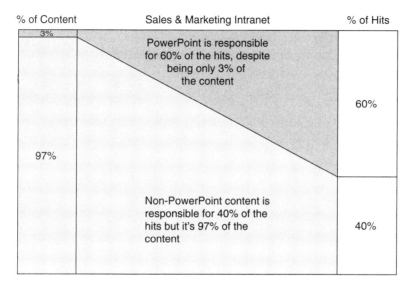

FIGURE 4.1 *HP STUDY ON POWERPOINT USAGE*

For example, HP recently did a study of their internal usage of PowerPoint. As Figure 4.1 so dramatically shows, although presentations made up only 3 percent of the content on their Intranet, PowerPoint presentations accounted for more than 60 percent of the hits.[1]

This growth of PowerPoint as a standard business communication vehicle is due to the proliferation of the technology, the maturation of users, and three important factors:

1. PowerPoint forces brevity, specificity, and clarity, all of which enhance the knowledge-transfer experience of the reader.

2. The graphics enable complex ideas and topics to be more clearly communicated.

3. The architecture of the PowerPoint software makes it very easy to modify and customize because it stores concepts and ideas in smaller, more logical chunks than a typical document. A white paper, for example, is a single, large, logical and physical object containing multiple facts, ideas, and messages in a flowing, sequential structure that is not easily modified. When

---

[1]Internal study conducted by Hewlett Packard, 2003.

those thoughts are transferred to and delivered through a PowerPoint presentation, on the other hand, the result is a collection of smaller, logical chunks that can be reassembled, modified, and reordered to be more relevant to a specific situation.

The bad news is that the enormous growth of PowerPoint, coupled with the ease of modification, has created a significant PowerPoint management problem for many B-to-B companies. Few companies understand the amount of wasted cost and effort that this unmanaged growth in PowerPoint has caused. As soon as multiple people need to use, share, and modify common slides, problems occur. As Figure 4.2 shows, people regularly copy or morph slides and presentations, creating multiple and often inconsistent versions of the message, which can confuse salespeople and customers alike.

This morphing of PowerPoint slides not only increases the total volume of presentation content that's out there, but as we will see in a later chapter, it also has significant cost implications. People now have to deal with multiple versions of the same presentation, as well as morphed presentations scattered everywhere. This often causes confusion, wastes time, and hinders the delivery of consistent brand and value proposition messages, all of which exacerbate the size of the B-to-B Black Hole. What's more, the internal architecture of PowerPoint adds to the management problem. Even

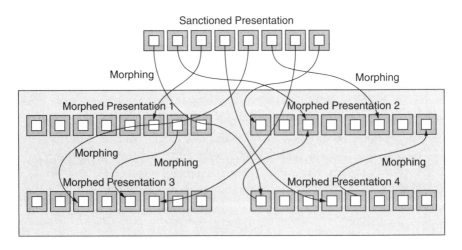

FIGURE 4.2 THE POWERPOINT MANAGEMENT PROBLEM

though PowerPoint is designed to make it easy for people to work with individual slides, its internal architecture has traditionally forced it to be managed at the presentation instead of the slide level. This restriction causes enormous amounts of presentation duplication and morphing in almost every marketing and sales organization.

MORE DYNAMICALLY CONFIGURABLE CONTENT

The second major trend that will change the B-to-B marketing and sales communication model forever are the advances in enterprise content-management technology that enable companies to manage content at a more granular and logical level. These advances allow for more customizable documents and Web sites, as well as more personalized and conversational interactions with visitors.

Componentization is one of the most important drivers of this new communication environment. As this trend develops over the next several years, it will enable salespeople to dynamically generate customized collateral, Web sites, correspondence, and even multimedia Flash™ presentations targeted to a specific selling situation or to the specific needs of prospects and customers. This ability to dynamically configure and re-use componentized content, including text and rich-media objects, will also allow B-to-B marketing organizations to exercise far more control over the quality of the information that is ultimately delivered to the customer, while allowing salespeople the flexibility to customize and fine-tune the content at the front lines, within certain parameters. This strategy of "managed flexibility" will considerably reduce the amount of morphing, duplication, and inconsistencies that reduces the content quality and drives the overall amount of content through the roof.

This new environment will also support a more conversational Web interaction model where, for the first time, B-to-B marketing organizations will be able to create more interactive Web sites that enable a substantive, two-way dialogue with prospects and customers. This new communication model will have a profound effect on the direct communications marketing organizations have with prospects and customers. It will require marketing professionals to think more like salespeople, however, and become adept at asking more substantive questions in a non-intrusive fashion so they can learn more specifics about the prospect's and customer's symptoms and business needs.

THE EVOLUTION OF COLLABORATION

The third trend impacting the B-to-B communications model is the adoption of collaborative technologies, including instant messaging, blogs, and Web meetings.

Instant messaging is a minimally intrusive way of increasing proximity and staying in touch. On the surface, it doesn't seem to interrupt people's workflow and productivity as much as a phone call does, and, as a result, I have begun to see an expanded use of instant messaging for sales and sales support activities. During the summer of 2004, studies of the instant message traffic on Yahoo, AOL, and MSN showed that 30 percent of the instant messages flying through cyberspace were from business people, and that 40 percent of these messages led to follow-up phone calls.[2] There is no doubt that this technology will become pervasive in business environments as more and more people stay online throughout most of the day.

Weblogs, better known as blogs, are Web pages made up of short, frequently updated postings arranged chronologically like a discussion group or chat room. Because it's so easy to publish and add to blogs, they are proliferating and becoming an accepted way for small and reasonably large networks of people with similar interests to interact with each other and share their thoughts and ideas. In the fall of 2003, the National Institute for Technology and Liberal Education estimated there were more than 1,200,000 active blogs on the Internet.[3] Blogs are the epitome of the anarchy that is the essence of the World Wide Web, and there are blogs on almost every topic, where the thought leaders and the "man on the street" can share their ideas with each other in an open and unrestricted forum.

So, what do blogs mean to the B-to-B communication model? Even though the blogging phenomenon is nascent, it needs to be taken seriously. Some people are projecting that blogs will eventually replace e-mail marketing.

---

[2]Leslie Walker, "Instant Messaging is Growing Up and Going to Work," *Washington Post*, September 2, 2004.

[3]Study conducted by the National Institute for Technology and Liberal Education, October, 2003, cited in *Computerworld*, February, 2004.

Blogs also offer a great vehicle for collecting competitive insights and best sales practices. As such, marketing organizations should make an effort to monitor blogs of the thought leaders in their industry to find out what people are saying about their products and services. For example, many research firms—including Gartner, IDC, and Jupiter Media—have their analysts keep blogs on issues affecting the particular industries they study.[4] Secondly, blogs can be easy to set up for special projects and communities of interest within the sales channels and customer base, and they can be used by marketing and sales organizations to share ideas and create more of a presence with their prospects and customers. In fact, the American Marketing Association has recently announced a new educational initiative to train its members on how to use blogs in their marketing mix.[5]

Finally, during the last few years, the Web conferencing market has exploded for broadcast events, such as employee training and "Webinars." But it's also beginning to pay dividends for more narrow-cast communications, like internal meetings and complex customer support activities. This trend will only accelerate as bandwidth increases, telecommunications costs come down, and Web conferencing companies continue to upgrade their offerings, making them easier to use for smaller, more interactive Web meetings. It is very likely that Web meetings and presentations will ultimately replace a lot of the face-to-face sales and sales support calls that consume so much time and resources, thereby extending the length of the sales process.

As an example, a 2003 report by Collaborative Strategies reported that Microsoft "recognizes that e-meetings may be the next collaborative killer application . . . and over the next five years they expect to see e-meeting technologies become nearly as common as conference calls are today."[6] Microsoft's new service, Live Meeting™, which is a result of their acquisition of PlaceWare, will further accelerate this shift to Web conferencing as a

---

[4]"Blogs: Marketing Beyond the Web Site," AMA Hot Topic Series, http://www.marketingpower.com, December, 2004.

[5]http://www.marketingpower.com

[6]Microsoft Collaboration Strategy Industry Brief, published by Collaborative Strategies, Inc. (San Francisco, California: December, 2003).

primary communications and collaboration platform for substantive business interactions of all kinds, including sales calls and presentations. Microsoft is spending a lot of marketing money on radio, TV, and print to promote this service.

Web conferencing has already become a staple for a few B-to-B software companies that use it to do remote product demonstrations in the later stages of the selling cycle, as I discovered through my research for this book. According to Angela Teague of BMC, these Web demonstrations have significantly reduced travel costs and shortened the time it takes to close a sale, and she feels that these benefits are only the tip of the iceberg.

Brian Enright, a Vice President at Lawson Software, agrees. "We've achieved significant time savings and cost benefits by demonstrating our products through a Web meeting. Our next challenge is to move this technology upstream, and get our sales and sales support people to embrace Web presentations to increase their effectiveness in the early stages of the sales cycle and shorten the prospect qualification and education process."

This integration of collaborative technologies, including Web conferencing, into the selling process is all part of the evolution of the B-to-B communication environment, and I believe that Web meetings will soon become as prevalent as telephone selling has become for most sales organizations. The reason for this is pretty clear. The aggressive adoption of collaborative selling technologies will significantly shorten sales cycles, reduce selling costs, and eliminate waste by attacking some of the logistical complexity of the buying process. The beauty of Web-assisted sales calls and Web presentations is that they can also increase the overall quality of many of the sales interactions, and can differentiate and enhance the selling, as well as the buying, experience through:

- More subject matter experts and sales managers attending the meetings from their office.
- The ability to pre-record experts and customer quotes to be easily accessed and played during the sales call.
- More consistent delivery of the message because of the presentation media's structure.
- More buy-in of ROI scenarios because they were developed in a collaborative fashion.

WEB-ASSISTED SELLING

As a result of the growth in PowerPoint, more configurable content, and the emergence of collaborative technologies, a fundamentally new communication environment for B-to-B marketing and sales organizations is rapidly evolving. I call this new environment "Web-Assisted Selling." Web-Assisted Selling will require the blending of content management with the communications process in a more rational fashion so that the access and assembly of PowerPoint slides and other rich-media assets is more tightly integrated with the Web-conferencing platform. This will make the process of creating and executing a Web meeting so simple that salespeople will be able to do it on the fly.

This new, integrated content and communication model will need to be embraced in a way that promotes increased marketing and sales alignment, minimizes the effects of the B-to-B Black Hole, and supports a more robust and integrated knowledge-transfer environment. In this new environment:

- The use of PowerPoint and other rich media, such as Flash, will continue to grow, but these content assets will need to be managed in a more systematic and granular fashion to minimize morphing and duplication.

- Marketing organizations will have more interactive and richer two-way Web dialogues with prospects that will ultimately generate higher-quality leads. Marketing professionals will finally have the power of the question in their toolbox, and they will have to learn how to use this power effectively so they can have more substantive interactions with Web site visitors in order to generate higher-quality leads. However, since marketing professionals will have more of a voice throughout the entire selling process, they must also become more tightly aligned with their sales counterparts.

- Salespeople will be able to provide customized and personalized content to prospects and customers that is pre-approved by marketing, higher in quality, and more consistent with the brand strategy.

- Web-assisted sales and sales support calls will support guided selling processes, such as needs analysis, ROI scenarios, and especially Web presentations with integrated rich media and audio.

Like any new idea, this new communication model means that processes, as well as cultures, will need to change. This requires management vision and commitment. As with most paradigm shifts, the companies who get there first will grab the biggest rewards.

It wasn't that long ago that the concept of telephone selling was considered radical for B-to-B sales organizations. This new marketing and sales communication environment driven by Web-Assisted Selling will evolve in much the same way, but it will evolve in "Internet Time" because of the pressures of the economy and the fact that customers will demand it. B-to-B sales channels will have to aggressively embrace this new model, not only because it will save time, reduce costs, and eliminate duplication, but because it will also enhance the buying experience, saving the customer time and money as well. As Stacie Cooperman of Lawson Software told me, "Once customers experience a well-run Web presentation, they will realize this is the way they want to be sold to. The bar will be immediately raised for all competitors."

CHAPTER 5

Understanding the Disconnect

Tʜᴇʀᴇ's ᴀ ɢʀᴇᴀᴛ ǫᴜᴏᴛᴇ from Benjamin Franklin, made as the Revolutionary War was beginning, that directly applies to B-to-B marketing and sales organizations: "We must, indeed, hang together, or most assuredly we shall hang separately."

As we have seen in previous chapters, the loss of real opportunities in the new economy combined with increasing complexity, changing market dynamics, and the evolution of a new communications model require more effective and efficient marketing and sales execution (see Figure 5.1), especially during the early stages of the funnel. Specifically, it requires a much higher level of integration and alignment between marketing and sales organizations.

Fortunately, the issue of marketing and sales alignment is now getting more management visibility, and some industry analysts are starting to publish studies and reports on the debilitating effects of the marketing and sales disconnect.

For example, a recent report from the Aberdeen Group concluded: "Marketing often accuses sales and channel partners of underutilizing or misusing marketing collateral, while salespeople complain that the sales and sales support tools provided by marketing are hard to find or poorly tailored to their particular needs. Marketing is concerned about maintaining message consistency so as to sustain the brand, while sales is concerned with tailoring the message to close the deal. Finally, marketing needs to know what information and sales collateral will help close business, sales management needs to know that their sales personnel are following best practices, and both groups need to know how customers are responding to the firm's value propositions."[1]

---

[1]"Bridging the Great Divide: Process, Technology, and the Marketing/Sales Interface," research published by Aberdeen Group (Wellesley, Massachusetts: 2002).

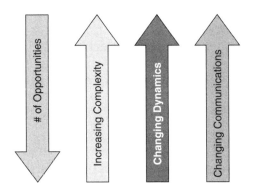

FIGURE 5.1 THE NEED FOR INCREASED ALIGNMENT

Another study published in 2002 by the Yankee Group, entitled "Improving Sales Effectiveness in a Down Economy," included a chart (Figure 5.2) that encapsulates the many misalignment problems B-to-B companies face on a daily basis.[2]

As this chart shows, there are a lot of different ways in which the marketing and sales disconnect rears its ugly head, and my research indicates that these are just the tip of the iceberg. For example, in 2000, I funded a study by Pragmatic Marketing of product marketing managers that found that 25 percent of all B-to-B marketing and sales budgets and resources were routinely wasted due to the inefficiencies and ineffective execution caused by misalignment and poor coordination.[3]

Because the symptoms of the marketing and sales disconnect are so far-reaching, a lot of executives still struggle with getting their hands around the problem. Few are able to discuss the symptoms of misalignment in a dispassionate and rational fashion so that they can effectively treat the disease. To help managers get past the emotional aspects of the disconnect, I came up with a simple way of viewing marketing and sales organizations as a single ecosystem made up of processes, assets, and activities, which are usually not as aligned as they need to be.

---

[2]Cheryl Kingstone, "Improving Sales Effectiveness in a Down Economy," a CRM Strategies Report, published by Yankee Group (Boston, Massachusetts: 2002).

[3]Study conducted by Pragmatic Marketing, 2002.

Sales' Perception	Marketing's Perception
Marketing never creates the precise information needed to close the deal.	We create hundreds of sales materials, but seldom receive feedback.
We are forced to create our own new customized content necessary for effective selling.	Sales never uses the approved materials, and as a result, inconsistent messages compromise the brand.
The new corporate marketing programs are late and hinder us in meeting our revenue goals.	We are creating programs as quickly as possible across all channels.
We can never find or get access to the content that marketing has created.	We are spending too much time on tactical selling activities such as sending out collateral.
We wish we were able to replicate certain messages that are resonating with the customer.	We wish we had more information as to "what works and what doesn't" in the field.
The leads we get are a waste of our time.	Why doesn't sales act on our leads?
We spend too much time searching for just the right information.	We spend too much time searching for just the right information.

Copyright 2002, the Yankee Group

FIGURE 5.2 CONFLICTING DYNAMICS BETWEEN SALES AND MARKETING

MISALIGNED PROCESSES

There are three macro processes that drive the generation of revenue for B-to-B companies:

1. The buying process
2. The marketing process
3. The selling process

Unfortunately, as Figure 5.3 indicates, in a lot of B-to-B companies these three macro processes often do not interface or align well with each other, causing considerable time delays and a lot of wasted effort and resources.

This misalignment of processes is best exemplified by the marketing and sales disconnects in the demand generation stage at the front end of the funnel that exacerbate the Event Horizon phenomenon I discussed earlier. The three flashpoints that drive misalignment in this area are the perceived quality of leads, the sales follow-up of leads, and the lack of constructive feedback from salespeople.

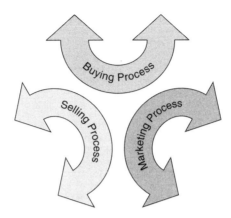

FIGURE 5.3 *MISALIGNED PROCESSES*

During my career, I have witnessed and participated in plenty of conversations on these three issues that go something like the following two scenarios:

Scenario One

Sales: The leads you provide are worthless!

Marketing: How do you know? You never call them!

Scenario Two

Sales: The leads you provide are worthless!

Marketing: How about ABC company? Didn't we provide you with the lead that resulted in that big sale you closed last quarter?

Sales: Nah, I was already aware of that opportunity.

Marketing: Yeah, right!

MISALIGNED ASSETS

While it's obvious that people are the primary assets of any marketing and sales organization, there are also some critical intellectual assets that drive all marketing and sales initiatives and activities. I call these the "Core Intellectual Assets," and they include the approved or Sanctioned Content as well as the institutional knowledge that drives the message and forms the foundation for that Sanctioned Content.

In reality, that institutional knowledge is the DNA of a company's value propositions and it is the raw material that drives all marketing and sales activities and deliverables. In today's businesses, much of this knowledge is often scattered throughout the enterprise. All companies have this embedded knowledge somewhere, but in too many cases it is like buried treasure, and marketing and sales organizations have not implemented the processes to document and effectively leverage this critical asset. As a result, a lot of the golden nuggets that make up this critical knowledge are never documented. Instead of being institutionalized so they can be leveraged in a systematic fashion, they are shared around the watercooler or through phone conversations and e-mail on an ad-hoc basis, if they are shared at all.

As you can see from Figure 5.4, the Core Intellectual Assets of a marketing and sales organization are made up of two things—knowledge assets and Sanctioned Marketing and Sales Content.

Knowledge assets include:

1. The different elements of a company's value propositions, including the facts, opinions, and insights on how their products and services intersect with and address the needs of their prospects and customers, hopefully in a way that differentiates them from the competition. As I mentioned previously, these individual elements are in reality the DNA of these value propositions, and I am convinced that this Value DNA needs to be managed in a more systematic fashion.

2. The raw knowledge behind the best sales practices for:
   - Generating interest
   - Understanding and developing needs
   - Delivering the messages and overcoming objections
   - Moving the selling process to the next stage
   - Laying traps for, and responding to, the competition

Sanctioned Marketing and Sales Content include a company's:

- Customer-facing promotional material and marketing collateral used to establish and reinforce the brand, generate leads, and deliver the value propositions to the marketplace.
- Presentations and selling tools, such as needs analysis systems, cost justification and ROI models, product configurators, and proposal generators.
- Training content and other internal content used to train employees and channel partners.

Unfortunately, as Figure 5.4 indicates, both the underlying knowledge and the Sanctioned Content that make up these Core Intellectual Assets are

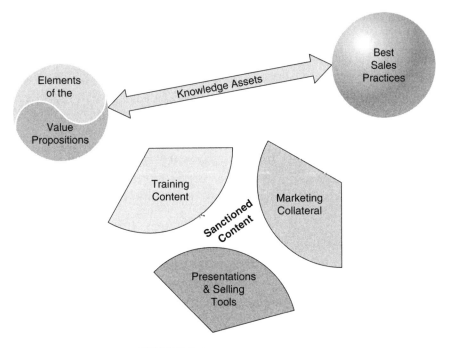

FIGURE 5.4 *MISALIGNED ASSETS*

rarely managed in a coordinated or integrated fashion. Thus, they are often misaligned with each other.

Because of this misalignment, the Sanctioned Content often doesn't reflect and is out of sync with the best organizational knowledge. Additionally, the three different areas of Sanctioned Content often contradict each other.

When these intellectual assets are misaligned, there is little sharing of critical information, the sales channels make little use of the content and collateral that marketing creates, and marketing gets little constructive feedback from salespeople. All of this exacerbates the marketing and sales disconnect and increases the magnitude of the B-to-B Black Hole, especially in the early stages of the marketing and selling process.

MISALIGNED ACTIVITIES

Because most of the things that marketing and sales professionals do on a daily basis are driven by their company's processes and the Core Intellectual Assets, the misalignment of processes and assets increases the misalignment of day-to-day activities. The most visible example of this phenomenon is the lack of coordination between what I call the three "Critical Communications Activities" that are fundamental to any successful marketing and sales organization:

1. The positioning and branding programs and activities run by marketing
2. The demand and lead generation activities performed by marketing
3. The sales and support activities, which include the interactions, conversations, and correspondence that sales and support people have with prospects and customers

As Figure 5.5 indicates, in many B-to-B companies these Critical Communications Activities are not well integrated or aligned. The branding message and positioning activities are not consistent with the lead generation strategy, and both of these are inconsistent with what the sales and sales support people tell their prospects and customers on a daily basis. In other words, marketing and sales rarely speak with a single voice, and this can cause a lot of wasted motion that often confuses prospects and customers. Once again, a lot of time and energy are lost to the Event Horizon that occurs in the front half of the funnel.

FIGURE 5.5 *MISALIGNED ACTIVITIES*

Another phenomenon that contributes to the misalignment between these activities is the issue of "account ownership." While it's important for salespeople to feel a strong sense of responsibility toward their customers, the new communications model I described in the previous chapter demands that salespeople get much more comfortable with their customers being "touched" by marketing throughout all stages of the sales funnel. The customer belongs to the company, not the salesperson, and salespeople who try to control every customer interaction will only foul up the works.

MISALIGNED VALUE ORIENTATION

I contend, however, that the primary cause of the misalignment between marketing and sales processes, assets, and activities is the inability of many companies to systematically institutionalize the knowledge that makes up all their different value propositions. Value propositions are the heart of marketing and sales, but in many B-to-B companies this "heart" is not pumping as well as it should be. Holden Corporation, one of the leading B-to-B sales training companies, recently completed a five-year study with more than 1187 participants (460 from sales and 727 from marketing). They concluded that the primary disconnect between marketing and sales organizations is the ineffective creation, validation, and delivery of the value proposition messages.[4]

After spending a lot of time talking to people about more systematic message management and the issues surrounding multiple value propositions, I have become convinced that too many managers underestimate their people's understanding of all the different issues and needs their customers face and all the different ways their products and services actually deliver value. If you think about it, there is a natural order of the logic needed to create relevant value propositions:

1. First, you need to have a detailed understanding of the different needs of stakeholders and customer constituencies from their perspective.

2. Next, you need to fully understand how stakeholders use particular products or services to solve their specific problems.

---

[4]"Marketing Alignment Benchmark Study," published by Holden Corporation (Hoffman Estates, Illinois: 2001).

3. Only after you understand these two aspects can you create complete and compelling value propositions for all stakeholders and customer constituencies.

In my experience, most companies don't have a systematic message development and management process that institutionalize these three steps. I have also observed that a lot of marketing and sales organizations often get into "messaging mode" long before there is a consensus regarding the specifics of the customer's need and the way value is derived. As a result, the message that is ultimately developed is too general, soft, and incomplete.

One of the fundamental conclusions of this book is that companies need to take more of an outside-in (customer- or needs-focused) approach vs. an inside-out (product- and feature-focused) approach to developing and communicating the value proposition messages for their solutions. The distinction between inside-out and outside-in is whether you approach value from an "it's about me" or an "it's about you" perspective:

- Inside-Out: "Here is my product or service. Look at all the neat things it has. Now, let's see if you need it."
- Outside-In: "Let me understand your business and your specific issues and needs, so we can both figure out whether or not my company can help."

Throughout this book, I will use the yin-yang model found in Figure 5.6 to represent the genetic structure of value propositions, or Value DNA. In this view, the value that is generated is represented as the intersection of products

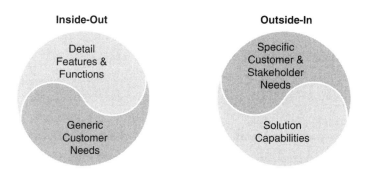

FIGURE 5.6 *INSIDE-OUT VS. OUTSIDE-IN*

and services and customer needs. This graphic also shows the difference between an inside-out and outside-in orientation. Specifically:

- An inside-out orientation starts with the assumption that salespeople, customers, and stakeholders intuitively understand the value of features. As a result, product features are on top, driving the communication of the value proposition. Most of the information on customer needs is broad and generic in nature, with little about the specific details of the customer needs.

- An outside-in approach, on the other hand, puts the customer and the stakeholders on top, focusing more attention on the specific details of their individual business issues and needs. When solutions are discussed, they are done so in terms of "how" the capabilities of the products and services solve those specific customer and stakeholder needs instead of "what" the different features are.

Taking an inside-out approach leads to what I call the reverse-engineering of the value proposition. Talking about features first invariably means you will discuss things that are irrelevant to the prospect, and he or she will tune out. It is nearly impossible to arrive at a relevant, compelling value proposition this way. But by taking an outside-in approach, getting agreement on the problems first, you eliminate this risk and generate true value propositions. Prospects see themselves in the marketing collateral and selling interactions, and know that your company "gets it" and is truly interested in solving their problem. As Jim Burns, the CEO of Avitage!, told me, "Only customers can call it a solution!"

Gerhard Gschwandtner, the publisher of *Selling Power Magazine,* told me that when he runs a Webinar for a vendor, he sends out two different e-mail invitations. One invitation takes an inside-out focus on the product, while the other takes an outside-in focus and doesn't mention the product at all. The outside-in e-mail usually generates three times more attendees for the Webinar than the inside-out e-mail.

So, with all of the evidence on the benefits of an outside-in approach, and the billions companies have spent on training salespeople to sell solutions, why do most B-to-B marketing and sales organizations continue to discuss their value propositions from the inside out? There are several reasons:

1. First and foremost, customers really do want to know about the features of products and services, and they send out mixed signals. In survey after

survey, they say they want salespeople to take the time to understand their needs, but they rarely give them the chance to do that. The first thing they say when they meet a salesperson is, "Tell me about your products," and the first thing they hit on a Web site is the products and services page.

2. Second, it's easier and more natural for marketing and salespeople to take the inside-out approach. It's human nature for most of us to talk and write about tangible things we're comfortable with. In marketing and sales, those things are usually the features and functionality of products and services, not necessarily the intricate details of a specific customer's needs.

3. Finally, the inside-out approach is easier to implement and scale from a content creation, sales training, and marketing communications standpoint. There is a well-accepted feature-and-function benefit structure for product-focused information that is not conducive to articulating the needs of individual stakeholders.

Salespeople make more of a conscious attempt to go outside-in in their conversations with prospects and customers, which is another contributor to the disconnect with marketing. There are three primary reasons for this:

1. Salespeople are organized around the customer, and they spend most of their time dealing with the specific needs of different stakeholders.

2. Salespeople have been formally trained in solution-centric selling, which reinforces the outside-in approach.

3. Salespeople have always had the most powerful communication technique ever invented in their arsenal—the question. Questions yield the give-and-take that helps salespeople work their way in from the outside.

Even with this extensive training and the power of questioning, the natural pressure to tell someone about all the neat features of a product or service is often too much for salespeople to resist. This pressure drives salespeople into what the management of Cisco calls "Spray and Pray Mode" or what the EDS folks call "Show Up and Throw Up."

There was a very interesting study done on B-to-B product launches in the late 1990s by the University of North Carolina. In confirming this phenomenon, the study uncovered some interesting things about the dangers of taking an inside-out approach to value:

• Salespeople asked 40 percent fewer questions on sales calls in which they introduced new products.

- Two out of three new products in the study failed to meet revenue expectations.

- The level of the sales channel's excitement about the new product had no relationship to the success of the new product rollout. What is interesting is that the more excited they were about the product, the fewer questions they asked and the less effective they were.[5]

As I mentioned earlier, salespeople have a distinct advantage over marketing people in balancing inside-out with outside-in communications, yet they still get it wrong a lot of the time. Most B-to-B marketing organizations, however, rarely go outside-in. Unlike their sales counterparts, marketing organizations:

- Are usually organized around products, and the job of a product marketing organization is to "give the product life."

- Rarely send their people on customer calls to experience the realities of selling.

- Have traditionally been brought into the solutions-selling training programs conducted for the sales channels.

- Until recently, never had "the question" in their arsenal. (The new Web based communications environment changes this, but most marketing organizations are still learning how to ask Web-based questions in a way that gets them relevant answers.)

- Historically, only had paper to work with. Since it was too expensive to design, create, and produce a unique piece of collateral for every stakeholder and specific business need, marketing was unable to get into too much detail on specific customer or stakeholder needs. Thus, B-to-B marketing departments have traditionally focused on broad, generic need messages for the theoretical customer combined with detailed product and feature information.

In 2000, Pragmatic Marketing, the leading provider of training for product managers, did an interesting study of more than 200 marketing professionals. It substantiated this tendency to think inside-out. While only 57 percent of these marketing professionals felt salespeople needed to know more about their customer's need, a full 98 percent of them felt salespeople

---

[5]Steve Sarno, Alston Gardner, and Jay Klompmaker, "Impact Marketing Research: Winning the Product Launch," research published by the University of North Carolina (2000).

needed to know more about their products.[6] This is exactly the opposite of what all of the customer research on this subject shows—that customers overwhelmingly want salespeople to know more about their needs!

Ultimately, marketing organizations must deal with the reality that customers and salespeople want specificity as well as clarity. Salespeople seldom deal with theoretical customers. They have been trained to ask more and more detailed questions and to focus deeper and deeper on the specific stakeholder's needs from the outside in. Meanwhile, marketing professionals, by the very nature of the tools they've had to work with, have been forced into telling the value story at either a very high level through brand messaging, or from an overly detailed, inside-out perspective designed to cover everything for every business need and stakeholder.

This basic disconnect between how salespeople and marketing professionals approach the value proposition significantly increases the misalignment between the two organizations. It impacts the quality of the Core Intellectual Assets and the execution of the Critical Communications Activities, and I contend that it's the biggest factor in the growth of the B-to-B Black Hole. Fortunately, the Value Mapping process I describe in Part II solves this problem forever. It provides a simple best practice that helps companies map all their Value DNA, and institutionalize a common and in-depth understanding of value throughout the sales and marketing organization so that the message is consistently reflected in everything both of them say and do.

SHIFTING EMPHASIS

In addition to the misalignment of the activities, processes, and the intellectual assets and the confusion over the creation and delivery of the value proposition messages, there has also been a slow shift in marketing's emphasis over the last two decades that has fueled the disconnect with salespeople. The evolution of the Internet and the increased sophistication of broadcast e-mail systems have accelerated the change in emphasis in many marketing organizations from sales support to demand generation over the last several years. Now that the Web has become marketing's primary

---

[6]Study conducted by Pragmatic Marketing, 2002.

content delivery vehicle, they are able to collect leads from their Web sites and can interact more directly with prospects and customers. As such, many B-to-B marketing organizations altered their marketing model and became more aggressive in their approach to demand generation during the last half of the 1990s.

While the Internet was becoming the primary marketing communications vehicle and the economy was going like gangbusters, the concept of managing the brand to gain maximum exposure migrated from consumer marketing, becoming a hot topic for B-to-B marketing management. As a result, in many companies during the late 1990s, marketing budgets and resources were directed away from traditional sales support activities and more toward branding and brand management initiatives. By the end of the twentieth century, many B-to-B companies were allocating more of their marketing budget and resources to branding and demand generation, and less of their resources to sales support activities, than they did only a decade ago.

As I mentioned earlier, the quality of the leads generated by marketing has always been an issue with the sales organization, and marketing and sales professionals alike often misunderstand the concept of branding. The fact that marketing organizations have shifted more emphasis and resources toward these two functions has caused the gap between marketing and sales to widen significantly in many companies over the last several years.

As the saying goes, "sales is like water, and it fills every gap." To counter this redirection of marketing resources, many companies created a whole new organizational entity called sales operations. Of course, this created additional marketing and sales infrastructure and cost. In many B-to-B companies today, sales operations is staffed with high-powered people who wield a lot of power and influence. In many cases, this new organization duplicates many of the activities done by marketing, which has actually increased the misalignment and further reduced the connection between what the marketing department produces and what sales channels actually use.

I contend that if marketing executives don't start making increased alignment with sales a central theme of their organizations, they run the risk of being marginalized. The good news is that many B-to-B marketing organizations have seen the light and are starting to re-allocate some of their resources from branding to lead generation. A 2004 survey from Bitpipe/SWMS found that 73 percent of companies plan to implement more online lead generation programs.[7] But unless the misalignment between the way marketing and sales approach value is corrected, and both organizations institutionalize an outside-in culture and approach to the marketplace, many of these leads will continue to be disregarded by sales-people. As a result, the B-to-B Black Hole will continue to grow, creating more waste and lost opportunities in the front half of the funnel.

---

[7]Study conducted by Sam Whitmore's Media Survey and Bitpipe, 2004.

CHAPTER 6

Strategic Mistakes

URING THE 1990S, when market share at any cost was the mantra, managers focused on scaling their people resources and doing more things faster. If you were a sales executive, each year you were handed a significant quota increase and additional headcount, and told to ramp up the channel capacity. If you were a marketing executive, you were given a bigger budget and asked to promote the brand and generate more leads. In the robust seller's market of the day, B-to-B marketing and sales had become a numbers game. Achieving scale was often more important than the quality of the day-to-day execution, and compressing the time it took to expand resources and activities was often more important than conserving cash.

All this changed almost overnight, however, when the economy turned south. From 2000 through 2003, many companies experienced what I call a "whipsaw effect," where the primary focus of many B-to-B marketing and sales executives shifted from scale to eliminating functions and resources as fast as they could. As the Aberdeen Group reported in early 2003, "Some of the marketing functions and activities in B-to-B firms have become expendable, as has been demonstrated by the dramatic retrenchment of marketing expenditures over the last 18 months."[1] Additionally, a comprehensive study by Hewitt Associates, a major HR research and consulting company, showed that 28 percent of the companies in the survey had recently reduced their sales forces.[2]

In times of extraordinary growth or severe retrenchment, it's often hard to focus on long-term effectiveness and productivity issues. I believe that

---

[1]"What Works: Best Practices in Marketing Technology: 21st Century Marketing Technologies Emerge," published by Aberdeen Group (Wellesley, Massachusetts, 2003).
[2]"Annual Report: Sales Force Retention," published by Hewitt Associates (Lincolnshire, Illinois: 2003).

many marketing and sales executives made three strategic mistakes during the last decade, mistakes that only exacerbated the marketing and sales disconnect and reduced long-term effectiveness:

1. They failed to understand that transferring knowledge was at the center of the marketing and selling process.
2. They failed to establish a true customer- and value-centric culture.
3. They failed to embrace quality management principles and processes.

THE IMPORTANCE OF KNOWLEDGE TRANSFER

In today's Information Age, knowledge drives the enterprise. If you think about it, marketing and sales is all about the efficient and effective acquisition and communication of facts, opinions, and insights in order to influence perceptions, attitudes, and behavior—in other words, transferring knowledge. Knowledge transfer is the very essence of the processes, assets, and activities of marketing and selling, whether it's accomplished through one-on-one conversations between salespeople and prospects, written correspondence, or broadcast communications such as advertising, Web sites, brochures, and Webinars.

When knowledge transfer is the ultimate objective, the give-and-take between marketing and sales professionals is more about what needs to be conveyed (the facts, ideas, and insights) than the precise words used to say it (the Sanctioned Content of the marketing collateral). This stimulates more substantive discussions that ultimately improve the relevancy and quality of the value propositions and other enterprise knowledge assets, and it fosters increased alignment. The reality, however, is that most of the arguments between marketing and sales organizations are over the words, which is often unproductive because that aspect is subjective and prone to personal prejudices.

This is why I believe that to be successful in the future, B-to-B marketing and sales executives must understand that, first and foremost, they are in the knowledge-transfer business. Once they accept this reality, their organizations can then work together to implement strategies and systematic processes that improve how their organizations gather, document, share, and leverage the knowledge that drives revenues and minimizes cost. As Lew

Platt, the former CEO of HP, said so eloquently, "If HP only knew what HP knows, we would be three times more productive!"[3]

When viewing marketing and sales as knowledge-transfer functions, it's important to remember that disseminating information is not transferring knowledge. When marketing and salespeople approach things from an information-dissemination perspective, they often measure success by how much content they publish and deliver. This is like measuring the effectiveness of an army by counting how many bullets were fired instead of whether or not they won the war.

This increased focus on knowledge transfer means that sales and marketing professionals need to see themselves more as educators and facilitators of the knowledge-transfer process, not just as lead generators or closers. Those who successfully make this transition will become part of the value their company provides, and they will significantly increase their company's overall value proposition in the eyes of their prospects and customers.

THE LACK OF TRUE CUSTOMER FOCUS

While almost every company was "talking the talk" about focusing on the customer, and a lot of sales organizations were trying to adopt solution-centric methodologies, most of the managers I talked to admitted that their marketing and sales organizations really weren't "walking the walk" in their day-to-day activities. After many discussions, I have concluded that a big part of the problem is that most of these companies have adopted a one-dimensional model for customer information.

In this single-dimensional information model (see Figure 6.1), which has been at the core of the Customer Relationship Management movement, attention is focused primarily on getting a better understanding of the historical sales transactions and service interactions a company has had with its customers.

Don't get me wrong; this historical orientation is important, and it has helped many companies significantly improve the customer focus in their

---

[3]"Three Proven Strategies for Better Knowledge Management," *CRM Magazine* Webinar, http://www.destinationcrm.com/webevents/details.asp?eventid=57, September, 2004.

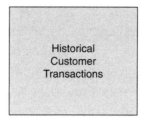

FIGURE 6.1 *SINGLE-DIMENSIONAL CRM MODEL*

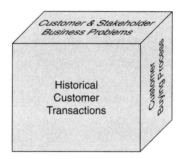

FIGURE 6.2 *THREE-DIMENSIONAL CRM MODEL*

service organizations. But I don't believe it has done a whole lot to make marketing and salespeople more customer-centric.

I contend that true customer-centricity requires a three-dimensional information model (see Figure 6.2). This type of model enhances the historical view of traditional Customer Relationship Management with two additional dimensions that help marketing and sales organizations institutionalize:

1. A detailed understanding of the specific issues and pains facing their prospects and customers, the individual stakeholders they sell to, and the marketplace in general.

2. A detailed understanding of how prospects and customers decide whether they are going to solve one of those business problems, and how they actually go about the buying process.

Even though most of the companies I talked to had implemented a CRM system to give them a more complete and accurate view of historical customer transactions, fewer than 10 percent of them had ever documented the specifics of their customer's decision-making and buying process, or formally aligned that process to the way they marketed and sold. Furthermore, more than 85 percent of the "C" level executives I interviewed for this book felt their marketing and sales organizations did not adequately understand the implications of their customer's business challenges and the specific value that their products and services provided to all the different stakeholders they sell to. As such, most of these executives felt their marketing and sales organizations were ineffective at consistently articulating a compelling value proposition to their prospects.

Obviously, a big part of this inability to effectively articulate value is driven by the disconnect between the inside-out and outside-in orientation that I spoke of in the last chapter. The other reason, however, is that a lot of marketing and sales executives feel the value of their products and services is obvious. While they all create some sort of positioning statement or document to codify their messages, they often underestimate the ability of their people to put themselves in the shoes of the customer, and they assume their prospects and customers intuitively understand all of the business issues and different implications of their value propositions. Because of this perception of "obvious value," few companies have a systematic process for developing and hardening all their value propositions, and most positioning documents end up being too broad and watered down.

As I mentioned in the last chapter, when you look at value propositions in their broadest sense, they are a compilation of the many facts, opinions, and insights (Value DNA) that sellers want to convey to the marketplace in order to describe and prove how their products and services have unique capacities to solve specific customer and stakeholder problems and needs. This knowledge, which I call the Value DNA, is usually sprinkled in lots of different places in an enterprise, and most companies do not have a process to identify and document these important facts, opinions, and insights. As such, their value propositions are often generic, and their selling discussions are not nearly as deep or precise as they need to be. In the end, all vendors start to sound alike, and there is little perceptible differentiation conveyed to the marketplace.

What is needed is a process to document and catalogue this Value DNA in much the same way genetic scientists mapped the human

FIGURE 6.3 COMPLETE VALUE PROPOSITIONS

genome. This would enable management to institutionalize a much more substantive understanding of the customer and stakeholder needs throughout the organization and develop more Complete Value Propositions. This process would not only identify and catalogue the broad business issues, but also the specific needs of individual stakeholders and how customers use the capabilities of a product or service to address these different business and stakeholder needs. Around this more detailed definition of value (as seen in Figure 6.3) would be the facts, opinions, and insights that allow marketing and sales professionals to have more relevant and intelligent conversations with their customers and answer the following tough questions:

- Show me that you really understand my business and my problem.
- How do I use your solution to solve my problem?
- How much is your solution worth to me, and how do I quantify that value?
- Can you prove that value?
- Why can your solution deliver more value than the other alternatives I have?
- Why do I need to act now?

In my estimation, companies with multiple products and services can have hundreds of these Complete Value Propositions, and they are some of those corporation's most important assets. Further, I believe that someone within the organization needs to formally own these knowledge assets, as well as the process to create and continuously improve and harden the messages. Yet, as I've mentioned before, almost none of the companies I contacted during my research for this book have ever organized these facts, opinions, and insights in one place so that their marketing professionals and sales channels could easily answer the above questions. In fact, many of them have never formally documented all their Value DNA at all. Instead of being leveraged in a systematic fashion, this critical knowledge was shared on an ad-hoc basis, if and when it was shared at all.

THE LACK OF QUALITY PRINCIPLES
AND PROCESSES

In the retail business, the key to marketing and sales effectiveness is "location, location, location." In the future, however, one of the mantras for B-to-B marketing and sales executives will be "quality, quality, quality." Not only will they need to focus on the quality of their human resource assets, but they must also focus on continuously improving the quality and impact of the Core Intellectual Assets and Critical Communication Activities in order to remain competitive.

The equation is really quite simple:
Quality People + Quality Intellectual Assets = High-Impact Activities

As complexity and the rates of change increase, the quality of the Core Intellectual Assets and Critical Communication Activities can often make the difference between the success and failure of a B-to-B enterprise. As such, the quality management principles that dramatically improved the effectiveness and productivity of the manufacturing sector over the past twenty years need to be applied to marketing and sales organizations. And, just as increased product quality required a tighter alignment between R&D and manufacturing, focusing on quality will require a lot more alignment and coordination between marketing and sales professionals.

In the manufacturing sector, continuously improving product reliability and functionality were the operational objectives that drove the quality movement forward. In B-to-B marketing and sales, however, where effective knowledge transfer and influencing perceptions, attitudes, and behavior are the ultimate goals, those operational objectives are:

1. Increasing the relevance, value, and impact of the Core Intellectual Assets.

2. Reducing the total cost of these assets by improving their integration, accuracy, and consistency.

3. Improving the execution and alignment of the Critical Communications Activities, both in terms of how quickly people acquire and absorb information, and how well that knowledge influences their thinking and ultimately their behavior. In other words:

   a. Getting the right information

   b. To the right person

   c. In the right context

   d. At the right time

   e. In a way that accelerates their comprehension, lengthens retention, and causes them to take action

To accomplish this, both the Core Intellectual Assets and Critical Communication Activities must be managed in a more coordinated and integrated fashion to create an effective knowledge-transfer environment where continuous quality improvement is built into the process. Implementing quality-centric processes, however, will require a substantial shift in thinking and culture. Executives will have to fight the conventional thinking that marketing and sales activities are more of an art than a science, and that the chaotic nature of the B-to-B environment makes it impossible to collect the kind of metrics that traditional Total Quality Management (TQM) programs such as Six Sigma are based upon.

While there are some differences in the way you drive and measure quality in a marketing and sales environment, there are several significant things worth mentioning about a more rigorous and systematic approach to quality in marketing and sales:

- Quality is usually pretty easy to recognize. This is especially true of the Core Intellectual Assets and Critical Communication Activities.

- Focusing on quality sends the right message to the people in the organization and to the marketplace. It is pretty easy to get the whole marketing and sales organization aligned behind a quality initiative because it's not threatening to anybody and because most people want to be associated with quality.

- Implementing quality processes can simplify the messages. Many marketing and sales messages have become far too complicated and, in many cases, convoluted and cumbersome. As one CIO recently told me, "I'll shoot the next salesperson who mentions orthogonal or heuristics." Complex messages hinder the sales process, make life more difficult for the channels, and confuse prospects and customers.

- Quality management processes not only improve revenues, they also eliminate waste, compress time, and reduce the total cost of marketing and sales. This top and bottom line impact is the reason the quality movement in the manufacturing process during the 1970s and 1980s was so successful, and these same benefits apply to increasing the quality of the marketing and sales assets and activities.

It is also important to note that ROI was difficult to measure in the early days of the quality revolution in the manufacturing sector. Management quickly figured out, however, that the marketplace easily perceived a lack of quality in a product, and that that perception significantly impacted sales results. I believe this paradigm holds true for a company's marketing and sales assets and activities as well. High-quality content and selling interactions will be perceived as added value by customers and prospects, and vendors who waste their time with low-quality content and low-value sales calls won't get another chance at bat.

B-to-B marketing and sales, like a lot of other things in life, is a game of inches, where even a marginal improvement in the quality of an intellectual asset or communications activity can make the difference between success and failure. This is due to the chaotic nature of the B-to-B marketing and sales environment and a fundamental principle of Chaos Theory known as "Sensitive Dependence On Initial Conditions." This concept states that even a small amount of change can drastically change long-term results. This phenomenon is more commonly known as the "Butterfly Effect"—in theory, the flutter of a butterfly's wings can start a chain reaction that can ultimately lead to a tornado halfway around the world.[4] Over the years, I have come to believe it's the little things that can often make the difference

---

[4]"Butterfly effect," http://en.wikipedia.org/wiki/Butterfly_effect, November, 2004.

between winning and losing, and I have found that the key competitive successes I had as a salesperson and manager happened because of things like saying just the right thing to just the right person at just the right time. This Butterfly Effect explains why even a little decrease in the quality of a Core Intellectual Asset or Critical Communication Activity can spell disaster, and why small improvements in the execution of the fundamentals can ultimately make the difference between the success and failure of a sales cycle or a marketing campaign.

THE IMPACT OF THESE STRATEGIC MISTAKES

I believe that this lack of focus on knowledge transfer, the inability to effectively manage the three dimensions of customer information, and the lack of quality-centric processes has eroded the overall quality of the leads generated by marketing and reduced the effectiveness of the average sales call, especially during the early stages of the selling process. All of these execution problems contribute to misalignment. They have a significant effect on productivity, and they contribute to the increasing size of the B-to-B Black Hole in a lot of companies.

CHAPTER 7

Missed Opportunities

IN ADDITION TO THE three strategic failures discussed in the previous chapter, I have identified five great operational opportunities to reduce complexity and increase the alignment and effectiveness of marketing and sales processes, assets, and activities that most marketing and sales organizations have failed to capitalize on. These missed opportunities are:

1. The way Customer Relationship Management has been implemented
2. The way the concept of branding has evolved
3. The way companies have implemented solution selling
4. The way sales support resources have been managed
5. The way content has been mismanaged

THE FAILURE OF CRM

The CRM movement presented marketing and sales organizations with a golden opportunity to increase their alignment and effectiveness. However, most companies failed to take advantage of this opportunity because of the single-dimensionality of the CRM data model that I mentioned in the last chapter, as well as four other factors:

1. Most major CRM vendors did not articulate a coherent marketing and sales effectiveness strategy, or develop the kind of software functionality needed to promote the sharing and leveraging of knowledge and best practices. Even now, most of them still don't get it. If you want to test this out yourself, just ask your CRM salesperson what his or her company's strategy is for aligning marketing and sales organizations and increasing customers' long-term marketing and sales effectiveness.

2. The benefits of CRM were often oversold and, unfortunately, too many marketing and sales executives viewed the CRM software as a silver bullet. As a result, many of them rushed into implementation before they had fixed their core processes, which is putting the cart before the horse. A 2004 survey done by the IBM Institute for Business Value found that less than

20 percent of CRM projects are viewed as successful, but that "the success rate can become as high as 80 percent through proper business process methodology and prioritization and a greater focus on the human factors that surround those processes . . . the softer elements of CRM."[1] Unfortunately, IT objectives and implementation issues often became more important than the business processes and cultural issues. In fact, a 2003 study by Harte-Hanks showed: "Most CRM initiatives were being controlled not by sales, marketing, or customer service, but rather by IT departments that may or may not be making decisions based on customer needs."[2]

3. Too many CRM implementations focused on controlling salespeople and turning them into data entry clerks instead of trying to save them time, make their lives easier, and help them become more effective. I have seen many sales processes implemented in CRM systems that were too onerous, from both a control and administrative perspective. As a result of this focus on control and data collection, the user interfaces were too complex and salespeople rejected the software. In fact, I have observed that sales reps who feel their CRM system is intrusive will work ceaselessly to subvert it. But as long as the salespeople continue to make their numbers, most managers won't kick up too much of a fuss.

4. In a lot of companies, the marketing and sales automation strategies are fragmented and disconnected. I have found many companies where marketing and sales had implemented systems from different vendors that ended up duplicating data, creating multiple information silos that further widened the gap between marketing and sales professionals.

The good news is that a lot of companies are beginning to realize that "simpler is better" when it comes to CRM. They also now understand that simple integrated systems for processes like lead tracking and pipeline management can align marketing and sales organizations around a common information flow, which makes them far more effective.

B-TO-B BRANDING BLUNDERS

During the last half of the 1990s, the concept of managing the brand became a hot topic, and a lot of B-to-B marketing executives jumped on the

---

[1]Joshua Weinberger, "The Five Key Differentiators Between CRM Failure and Success," *CRM Magazine,* http://www.destinationcrm.com, April, 2004.

[2]"Who's In Charge of CRM?," *Customer Relationship Management Magazine,* December, 2004: 12.

bandwagon. In doing so, they began to spend considerable resources and re-allocated some of their best people to the branding function. Unfortunately, the intricacies and complexities of B-to-B branding were often not well understood by many marketing professionals, and this led to serious disconnects and a lot of wasted time, money, and effort. For example, according to a 2003 survey done by PricewaterhouseCoopers, 67 percent of senior managers felt their companies have a well-defined brand, but only 33 percent felt their own people understood the brand and its values.[3]

I believe that some B-to-B branding initiatives actually increased the misalignment between marketing and sales organizations because critical resources were taken away from the demand-generation and sales support activities. Marketing organizations made what I consider to be the three blunders of B-to-B branding:

1. Many B-to-B marketers defined branding too narrowly as a corporate identity and communications function. As such, these marketing organizations spent their time and energy creating corporate style guides for content and pre-approved templates for PowerPoint presentations. These seemed like good ideas at the time, but many marketing organizations made things far too complex and went overboard in their efforts to "be complete" and control the salespeople. In many companies this over-exuberance resulted in two-inch-thick style guides, bureaucratic approval processes, and restrictive PowerPoint templates that were rarely followed by the sales and sales support people. As the channels ignored these standards and created their own content, some of which was inconsistent and amateurish, marketing people became more and more aggravated. Of course, when the marketing organization made a big deal about the strategic importance of the corporate identity program and tried to enforce these restrictive procedures, the sales organization rolled their eyeballs. When marketing couldn't tie these initiatives to revenue, it reinforced the salespeople's impression that the marketing organization was focusing on the wrong stuff and, worse, hindering their selling efforts with more administrative nonsense.

2. Many B-to-B marketing executives failed to fully comprehend the substantial role played by the sales channels in the brand experience. If you look at the great B-to-B brands like IBM, NCR, Xerox, and HP, it becomes

---

[3]Sean Callahan, "Marketing Pros Feel Undervalued," http://www.btobonline.com, June, 2004.

clear that channel execution played a major role in building the brand. In fact, several studies have concluded that 80 percent of the pre-sales and as much as 50 percent of the post-sales for B-to-B companies is delivered through the sales and sales support channels.[4] However, the value of the channel was often underestimated in the 1990s, and this mistake was compounded when many pundits predicted the Internet would "disintermediate" salespeople. As we are all now aware, this "death of a salesperson" scenario has not happened.

3. A lot of marketing organizations didn't clearly connect the brand message to the sales message and create what I call a "branding chain" that logically links the company's messages from the thirty-thousand-foot level to the three-foot level. On top of this disconnect, many marketing organizations failed to bring the channels into the branding process early enough or to educate them on the brand strategy so they could explain the new branding initiative to their customers in a cohesive fashion. Of course, not being able to explain the brand message effectively made the channels look uninformed and out of the loop to their customers. As a result, lots of salespeople dismissed the branding initiative or new tag line as just another ineffective marketing program and waste of money. Meanwhile, the marketing people's perception of the channel continued to erode because, in their eyes, the salespeople were just too stupid to get the subtle brilliance of the brand messaging they had developed.

Fortunately, many marketing organizations seem to have learned their lesson. As a recent study of more than 350 marketing professionals concluded: "Generating leads and closing sales have eclipsed branding/market awareness as the most important ways marketing organizations now measure their performance—a clear indicator of the trend towards more tactical activities."[5]

THE FAILURE OF SOLUTIONS SELLING

For the past several decades, B-to-B companies have been trying to get their salespeople to more intelligently discuss the business issues and problems their customers face and to package their products and services as solutions

---

[4]Customer Message Management Forums, conducted by the American Marketing Association, June 2002, September 2002, and December 2002.

[5]CMM Forum, http://www.marketingpower.com, November, 2004.

to those problems. To accomplish this, they have spent billions on rigorous sales training programs and proprietary, solutions-centric and consultative selling methodologies.

The solutions-selling movement represented a great opportunity for marketing and sales organizations to transform and align themselves around a more customer-centric and needs-driven approach to the marketplace. But, as reported in a study by McKinsey & Co. published in 2002, "Solutions selling has been perhaps the most overused buzzword of the last decade, yet 75 percent of the companies that attempt to implement a solution-selling methodology fail to return the cost of their investment."[6] During my career, I have had the opportunity to use or work closely with most of the major sales training companies, and I believe there were several factors contributing to this failure:

1. First, most of these sales training companies assumed their clients' sales and marketing people fully understood both their customers' and stakeholders' business issues and problems. Due to the complexity of today's business problems, this was often a false assumption. Without an in-depth understanding of the customer and stakeholder needs, it is virtually impossible to sell solutions. Additionally, few of the solutions-selling methodologies included a systematic process for identifying, documenting, and institutionalizing an in-depth understanding of those needs throughout the sales and marketing organization, meaning the entire solutions-selling initiative was often built on a weak foundation.

2. Second, while most solutions-selling methodologies discussed the customer's buying process, the emphasis was often on forcing that buying process into the methodology's specific selling model. Most of those models emphasized the approval and closing process, not the needs development process. This approach often worked well in the seller's market of the 1990s but that dog won't hunt in today's economy. Now, the customer is in control, and selling has to be about helping customers accelerate their buying process on their own terms.

3. Most of the questioning and communications models included in these methodologies were overly complex, rigid, manipulative, and unnatural.

---

[6]Chandru Krishnamurthy, Juliet Johansson, and Hank Schlissberg, "Marketing Solutions," McKinsey & Co. (Atlanta: 2003).

FIGURE 7.1 *TRAINING WITHOUT REINFORCEMENT*

As such, very few salespeople were able to execute these questioning models effectively, and in those rare cases when they tried to do it, they often sounded scripted and injected a sense of artificiality into the selling conversations.

4. There was little thought given to the fact that solution-centric selling requires the transformation of both marketing and sales. Marketing was rarely trained to support and reinforce the selling methodology through the content and selling tools they created, and the sales training was managed as an "event," not a journey. In fact, the whole solutions-selling initiative was looked at as a training initiative, not an organizational transformation initiative. Not surprisingly, it suffered from the endemic problem faced by traditional training programs shown in Figure 7.1.

Something else has always bothered me about the business models of these sales methodology companies: The more complex the proprietary questioning and communication methodology was, the more expensive the training tended to be, both in the number of days required and the cost per day. It didn't take me long to figure out that holding two days of training for a dozen salespeople at $2,500 per head was a pretty good way to make a living, and that a business model based upon sales training days might have as much to do with the complexity of the methodology as the stated goal of improving sales effectiveness.

Clearly, the money was in maximizing the sales training days, and since there are far more salespeople than marketing people, few companies invested in building a solution-centric content curriculum for marketing professionals. The economics of a training-centric business model also explains the lack of traditional consulting services available to help marketing organizations create more customer-centric content.

The tougher selling environment of the twenty-first century has been a reality check for these training companies. As selling gets tougher and the dysfunctional relationship between marketing and sales becomes more apparent, many of them are beginning to understand that solutions selling is more about business transformation and culture change than it is about sales training days. As a result, I predict these training companies will change their business model to include more consulting and follow-on coaching. They will also invest more resources and attention in the marketing department in order to help marketing professionals create better sales tools and more customer-centric, sales-ready content.

For example, Mike Bosworth, the father of the solutions-selling movement and founder of Customer Centric Systems, has recently written a new book called Customer Centric Selling. Bosworth's approach focuses squarely on solving the marketing and sales disconnect and enabling salespeople to have more effective situational conversations with their customers and prospects, which means:

1. Having an intimate understanding of the customer's problem

2. Asking relevant questions that reflect that understanding so you appear to be more credible

3. Understanding the implications of the answers so you can add value[7]

As more and more training companies follow Bosworth's lead and develop a more holistic offering for both marketing and sales organizations, I believe they must resist the temptation to:

- Drive the marketing and sales content around their proprietary questioning and communication model. If they don't resist this urge, the inherent complexity of that model will show through, resulting in sales prompters and questioning templates that are more complex than they need to be, manipulative in nature, and artificial when delivered by a human being.

---

[7]Michael T. Bosworth and John L. Holland, *Customer Centric Selling* (New York: McGraw-Hill, 2004).

- Recommend their customers create stand-alone, paper-based sales toolkits and selling guides that are more complex and onerous than they need to be. In the past several years, I have seen a lot of companies invest big bucks in the creation of professionally produced binders and toolkits that get put on the shelf, and are rarely used by salespeople because of their cumbersome nature. These toolkits quickly get out of date as the messages and the competitive landscape change.

THE MISUSE OF SALES SUPPORT EXPERTS

As products and services became more complex in the 1990s, many B-to-B companies began to increase their sales support staffs and increase the ratio of technical and industry support experts to salespeople. My research shows that more than 60 percent of companies are currently spending a higher percentage of their budgets on sales support staff than they did just a few years ago. This large sales support resource has become a major expense, significantly increasing the cost of sales.

The theory behind this investment was that salespeople would handle the selling process—from the front end through the qualification phase and well into the closing phase—on their own before bringing in one of these highly paid sales support experts. Once the prospect was well qualified and fairly well educated by the salesperson, the technical and industry support specialists would provide the additional expertise to knock out any competition and accelerate the closing process.

Yeah, right! The salespeople quickly figured out that these sales support people could do some of the heavy lifting for them during the qualification process and, more importantly, that these subject matter experts were, in reality, a key part of their company's overall value proposition. Naturally, most salespeople tried to get them involved with their prospects as soon as possible so they could demonstrate their capabilities, expertise, and value early in the process. This over-dependency on sales support in the front half of the sales funnel made many salespeople less effective at developing needs and qualifying prospects.

During the 1990s, when market share and scale were often more important than saving money, four- and six-legged sales calls became quite common. The practice of bringing in the subject matter experts early became institutionalized in many B-to-B companies, and these highly paid, valuable sales support resources were often used in an inappropriate fashion. They frequently became involved in situations where the prospect clearly wasn't close to being qualified, causing three significant problems:

1. Increased selling costs, because time and resources were wasted on non-productive activities

2. Real opportunities missed because these experts were consumed on the wrong opportunities

3. High turnover, as these expert resources became frustrated with their jobs and became harder and harder to retain

In 2000, I had Pragmatic Marketing, the largest trainer of high-tech product managers, conduct a survey of more than 200 product marketing and support specialists in companies of all sizes. This study found that 93 percent felt they spent too much time going over the basics with salespeople and customers and more than 80 percent felt they were not used effectively and were regularly brought into unqualified situations where their time was wasted.[8] Of course, some prospects and customers now demand this kind of early attention from the experts as a prerequisite, so some sales organizations have been forced to continue this costly practice.

KNOWLEDGE AND CONTENT MISMANAGEMENT

Because of the changing communications model I described in an earlier chapter, over the last decade, the Core Intellectual Assets have become more critical to the B-to-B marketing and selling process. But most marketing and sales executives, as well as the CRM and content management vendors, have failed to understand the true nature of marketing and sales content and the enormous impact these intellectual assets have on productivity. As a result, few companies manage their knowledge and content assets in a systematic and integrated fashion that reflects:

- The unique dynamics of marketing and sales content that drive both the volume and the turbulence

---

[8]Study conducted by Pragmatic Marketing, 2000.

- The importance of quality in the knowledge-transfer experience
- The total cost of marketing and sales content

TURBULENCE AND VOLUME Marketing and sales content, by its very nature, is turbulent to begin with, and it is almost always in a state of flux. Prior to the advent of electronic content, turbulence and volume could be controlled by the limitations of paper. In those days salespeople used the collateral and presentation materials that marketing gave them. The idea of channel-created collateral (with the exception of a few presentation foils, which took a lot of time and effort to create) was almost unheard of. With electronic documents and presentations, however, both the amount of Sanctioned Content as well as the Total Content created by marketing and sales professionals began growing at a chaotic and unrestrained pace.

The amount of Sanctioned Content is growing because:

- Much of today's information is more perishable than in the past due to the changing market and communications dynamics and the shrinking message shelf life discussed in an earlier chapter.

- Marketing organizations often think they are in the information-dissemination business instead of the knowledge-transfer business. Thus, many of them keep putting out new stuff, just to justify their existence. In fact, one of the marketing executives I interviewed for this book had developed what he called the "always be publishing theorem"—keeping his people busy to increase his job security.

- The Dueling Product Manager Syndrome, in which product managers compete with each other for the mental shelf space of the sales channels. Product managers are traditionally compensated by the revenue success of their products, and as such, they have to fight with each other for the mind share of the salespeople. The problem is, however, that these product managers often compete for this mind share by providing more and more content in order to merchandise their products to the channels.

- The inherent duplication that occurs between customer-facing content and internal content. In my research I found that almost 80 percent of the internal training content in most companies' intranets included either copies of the exact same stuff that was in the customer-facing collateral and Web site or the same facts, insights, and ideas written in a slightly different way for internal consumption.

The amount of Total Content, however, is often growing faster than the amount of Sanctioned Content in many companies because of:

- The lack of effective content management practices. These are needed to ensure that out-of-date content, especially PowerPoint slides, is removed and eliminated when necessary.
- The ability for any person to publish content to the Intranet. In many companies this has created an explosion in the number of unsanctioned content sources that contain duplicate and inconsistent content. Today, anybody can easily become an author and publisher, and in many companies this has lowered the overall quality of the content.
- The ease with which sales and sales support people can modify or morph Sanctioned Content, as well as create their own content from scratch. As I mentioned earlier, this is especially true of PowerPoint presentations. For example, HP has found that more than 80 percent of the PowerPoint slides used by the sales and sales support channels were created or modified in the field, even though the company has a significant central library of "pre-approved" presentation material.[9] While there are some benefits to having the ability to customize presentation content for specific sales situations, sales and sales support people creating their own presentations and sales collateral consumes lots of time and costs lots of money. The process of this field-generated and "morphed" content also significantly increases the amount of duplicate and inconsistent information. Often, when a salesperson finds something that works, he or she passes it on, only to have it morphed again and again, so that different incarnations end up in lots of different places. Channel-created content also creates a huge quality-control problem and message and brand consistency issue for the marketing organization, which in turn increases the friction and widens the disconnect between marketing and salespeople.

Along with this enormous growth in the amount of both Sanctioned Content and Total Content, there is often a dramatic increase in the number of external and internal Web sites and newsletters a company has. Some of the Fortune 1000 companies I talked to as I was writing this book have more than a hundred Web sites for their salespeople and channels to wade through for information. One company I talked to also admitted to having more than sixty-two internal marketing and sales newsletters, each pushing a different product or service line.

---

[9]Study conducted by Hewlett Packard, 2003.

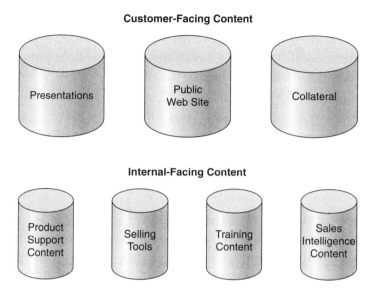

FIGURE 7.2 MULTIPLE CONTENT SILOS

This unrestricted growth in the amount of Total Content and the number of different content sources, or "silos," that inevitably follow (see Figure 7.2), has overwhelmed many salespeople, making it difficult for them to find the things they need when they need them. Of course, salespeople blame marketing for this overload, even though the salespeople themselves are responsible for much of the duplication and confusion. After all, the salespeople create a lot of the content and they drive almost all of the content morphing that occurs. This often creates further friction and widens the disconnect between the two organizations.

I did find a few larger companies who were trying to address this problem through the implementation of a single sales and marketing portal. Unfortunately, most of these were still struggling with developing an appropriate taxonomy to organize and tag all this content so it could be accessed in a way that reflected the way salespeople worked. A study by the CMO Council in June of 2004 confirmed this problem, stating that only 20 percent of the companies in the survey felt they did a good job at developing a taxonomy that effectively organized their content.[10]

---

[10]Bill Glazier, "Making Marketing Messaging Meaningful," published by the CMO Council (Palo Alto, California: June 3, 2004): 2.

THE IMPORTANCE OF QUALITY As I mentioned in a previous chapter, the whole notion of quality takes on a different perspective when you look at marketing and sales content as a knowledge-transfer vehicle rather than an information-dissemination vehicle. This knowledge-transfer perspective forces you to focus on the raw knowledge assets as well as the completed documents and presentations that make up the Sanctioned Content. It emphasizes whether the value messages are compelling, how well those messages are delivered through the content, and how well that content influences the perception, attitudes, opinions, and behavior of the reader.

There are two primary dimensions to consider in assessing the quality of marketing and sales content from a knowledge-transfer perspective—the value of the material and the impact of the delivery experience. Regarding the value of the material, companies should ask:

1. Is the content in context and pertinent to the reader?
2. Is the content current, accurate, and consistent?
3. Is the content—whether text, graphics, or rich media—clear and concise?
4. Does the content simplify things for the reader?
5. Does it have a structure that facilitates understanding, updating, and continuous improvement?

Regarding the impact of the delivery experience, consider:

1. Is the information easy to find and access?
2. Is the production quality professional and polished?
3. Do readers feel they are being dealt with in a more personalized and human fashion?
4. Does the interaction engage the reader and promote comprehension and retention?
5. Can the content be easily customized and re-purposed by the reader?

As I mentioned earlier, most companies have failed to grasp the importance of the knowledge-transfer perspective and this lack of understanding has been compounded by both the CRM and the Enterprise Content Management (ECM) vendors. I believe these companies have clearly dropped the ball on the marketing and sales alignment and effectiveness issue over the last decade. Both of these types of software companies provide marketing and sales content management solutions, but neither of them have ever aggressively embraced the idea that more integrated knowledge, content, and communications processes could significantly improve marketing and sales alignment and productivity. And from my perspective, most of them still don't get it! CRM companies think of content and knowledge management as an afterthought, and ECM vendors inevitably attack content management from the perspective of librarians, positioning themselves as IT infrastructure.

These software vendors also place way too much emphasis on technology, and while they all still talk about business transformation, CRM and ECM software have in fact become commodities in many respects. Merger activity, like the acquisition of Documentum by EMC, a company that makes storage devices, further demonstrates the IT infrastructure and commodity mentality of these Enterprise Content Management vendors.

THE TOTAL COST OF CONTENT The unrestricted growth of marketing and sales content, whether sanctioned or unsanctioned, plus the lack of quality-centric processes that support the creation and management of the knowledge and content assets have created a major undocumented expense item in many companies, which I call the Total Cost of Content. I contend that this Total Cost of Content is becoming more significant to B-to-B marketing and sales organizations as their intellectual assets play an ever-increasing role in the buying, selling, and sales training process.

The Total Cost of Content has two dimensions that are sometimes difficult to measure, but by all accounts are rapidly becoming major cost, time, and productivity drains on both marketing and sales professionals alike:

- The Visible Cost, which includes all the time and resources that marketing, training, and sales operations departments spend on creating and managing the Sanctioned Content.
- The Invisible Cost, which includes:
  1. The enormous amount of time spent by salespeople who roll their own content, either because they can't find what they are looking for, they don't like or trust what marketing has provided, they need to customize

some existing content to personalize it for a specific prospect or customer situation, or they just feel the need to be creative and do their own thing.

2. The time and energy it takes for salespeople, prospects, and customers to wade through the incorrect, out-of-date, duplicate, and morphed content so they can ultimately access the appropriate information. There are several studies indicating that as much as 80 to 90 percent of the material produced by B-to-B marketing organizations is considered irrelevant and not used by the channels. Additionally, some studies have documented that as much as 40 to 60 hours of a typical salesperson's month are taken up by re-creating, often badly, specific customer and stakeholder collateral and presentations. Other studies have concluded that the average knowledge worker spends 2.5 hours per day searching for the right information, and several white papers I have read over the last few years indicate that in some industries the average B-to-B salesperson spends as much as one day a week just looking for and assembling content that contains the information they need.[11]

3. Lost revenue from valid sales opportunities that fall through the cracks while salespeople, customers, and prospects act on incorrect or outdated information.

4. Delays in revenue when sales cycles are elongated and new product roll outs are stymied by inconsistent, out-of-date, and just plain erroneous content.

5. The revenue lost due to extended sales ramp-up times while salespeople try to rationalize all the different sources of content.

In many companies, most of the Invisible Costs have gone unnoticed because they are not readily identifiable and because most sales and marketing executives are buffered from many of the frustrations surrounding content that their people deal with on a daily basis. One of the things I discovered from my research, for example, was that a lot of these executives were unaware of how bad the PowerPoint problem had become in their organizations because they had assistants who did their PowerPoint presentations for them.

---

[11]Proceedings of the Customer Message Management Forums, published by the American Marketing Association and Ventaso, 2002 and 2003.

THE CONTENT CONUNDRUM

When you look at all the factors that make up the Total Cost of Content, you end up with a phenomenon I call the "Content Conundrum." Although it's very difficult to precisely measure the impact of this Content Conundrum, most of the marketing and sales executives I talked to agreed, after reflecting on all the issues, that it was indeed a significant problem. The underlying dynamic that drives this problem is the fact that the amount of Total Content is growing faster than the amount of Sanctioned Content. There are two major reasons for this:

1. As the amount of Sanctioned Content grows, it becomes increasingly difficult to maintain the currency and accuracy of that content, so errors, inconsistencies, duplicate, and outdated information creep in. In my research I was unable to find even one company who claimed to have cracked the code on this issue. More importantly, in every discussion I had on this topic, the person I was talking to concluded that even if it were physically possible to keep the Sanctioned Content accurate and up-to-date, the cost and manpower required to do so would be unacceptable.

2. As the amount of Sanctioned Content grows, it spawns an enormous amount of content morphing, especially of presentation content, by the sales channels so the amount of total content grows almost exponentially.

Because the amount of Total Content is often growing at a faster rate than the Sanctioned Content, the Invisible Costs of Content are almost always growing faster as well. Figure 7.3 clearly shows why the Content Conundrum has evolved into a significant problem for many B-to-B companies, and why it could potentially become one of the biggest long-term operational problems facing marketing and sales organizations.

So . . . let's see if I get this straight:

- The amount of Sanctioned Content is growing at an ever-increasing rate as markets and products change and become more complex.
- Because of the amount of content morphing, sales-created collateral, redundant and duplicate content, and out-of-date information, the amount of Total Content in most companies is growing faster than the amount of Sanctioned Content. In fact, the Total Content line could theoretically go asymptotic, heading off the chart if this problem is not addressed in a systematic fashion.

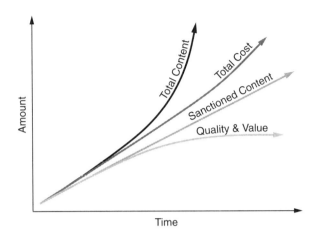

FIGURE 7.3 THE CONTENT CONUNDRUM

- The Total Cost of creating, maintaining, and using all of this content, when you add in both the Visible and Invisible Costs, often grows at a faster rate than the amount of Sanctioned Content.
- Finally, because of the way content is mismanaged, the average quality, accuracy, and currency of the company's content assets erode over time. As the Quality and Value line at the bottom of the graph indicates, each day the amount of Sanctioned Content and Total Content grows, it actually loses some of its value.

So, the more we create and the more we invest, the worse it gets! I don't know of any other corporate asset that behaves in this manner, and it sounds like a train wreck to me!

Unless companies establish a long-term vision for their marketing and sales knowledge and content, and make fundamental changes in the way they manage these Core Intellectual Assets, it's only going to get worse. In a lot of the B-to-B companies I encounter, the Content Conundrum has already become a debilitating problem, and in some cases, it has become the single biggest barrier to improving overall marketing and sales productivity and effectiveness.

I contend that the combination of the five missed opportunities and the three strategic failures discussed in the previous chapter have measurably increased the disconnect between marketing and sales. This increased misalignment has often reduced the quality of the execution of some of the fundamental marketing and sales activities in many companies, at a time when effective execution is required for survival. Together they have created a fertile environment for the development and continued growth of the B-to-B Black Hole.

Fortunately, there is an answer. Management needs to take the B-to-B Black Hole seriously and make marketing and sales alignment a core strategy of their go-to-market model.

PART II

CLOSING THE GAP

"The boundary between sales and marketing is becoming so blurred that the distinction is no longer helpful."

—GEORGE WEATHERSBY, CEO OF THE AMERICAN MANAGEMENT ASSOCIATION[1]

---

[1] *Sales & Marketing Management Magazine,* Fall, 1998.

CHAPTER 8

Alignment as a Core Strategy

A S WE HAVE SEEN THROUGHOUT PART I, the increasing complexity and hyper-change in the marketplace, combined with a growing misalignment between marketing and sales organizations, has created a Black Hole in many B-to-B companies where significant costs, resources, and time are wasted, and viable opportunities are missed and lost forever. And as we have seen, the symptoms of the Event Horizon of this Black Hole are many:

- 70 to 80 percent of the leads generated by marketing are never followed up.
- Only 29 percent of a salesperson's time is actually spent selling.
- 80 percent of sales support experts are regularly used inappropriately.
- 75 percent of solutions-selling initiatives have failed to generate any ROI.
- More than 80 percent of marketing and salespeople can't consistently and effectively articulate their value propositions.
- 80 to 90 percent of marketing collateral is considered useless by sales.
- Salespeople typically spend 30 to 50 hours per month searching for information and re-creating customer-facing content.
- 80 to 90 percent of the customer-facing content created by salespeople is inaccurate and dilutes the brand.

Marketing and sales organizations, by the very nature of what they do and the complexity and change they deal with, will always incur some amount of waste and inefficiency. But marketing and sales executives can no longer afford to ignore these symptoms, as many of them did in the 1990s. The economic and competitive realities of today's markets have created an environment where marketing and sales disconnects can have a significant impact on both the top and bottom line performance of an enterprise:

- 50 percent of salespeople are not achieving their sales quotas.
- 70 percent of new product launches fail to meet initial expectations.
- 90 percent of sales opportunities don't close as forecasted.

The challenge for management, however, will be to act like a good doctor, focusing on the underlying disease and not just the individual symptoms. To escape the B-to-B Black Hole successfully, managers need to get at the root of the marketing and sales disconnect and create a Synchronized Marketing and Sales Ecosystem that is truly focused on the customer. I believe there is a whole lot management can do to facilitate this ecosystem, and most of it is pretty simple. All they need to do is to take the misalignment threat seriously, and make improving marketing and sales alignment a central principle of their company's:

- organizational strategy
- compensation and recognition programs
- operational processes

Looking at marketing and sales effectiveness through this lens of alignment will provide management with a greater sense of clarity on some of the day-to-day execution issues that can make a difference in both the top and bottom line. Creating a Synchronized Marketing and Sales Ecosystem will enable them to increase revenues, reduce the total cost of marketing and sales, and create sustainable competitive advantage.

ALIGNMENT-CENTRIC ORGANIZATIONS

While every company needs to look at its organizational strategy in the context of its own unique business model and culture, I did find a few common best practices during my research that were helping management in several companies increase alignment, improve overall effectiveness, and reinforce the vision of a Synchronized Marketing and Sales Ecosystem.

On the surface, it might seem that the organizational issues surrounding alignment are pretty simple. If you want to increase the integration between sales and marketing, have them both report to a single Chief Marketing and Sales Officer (CMSO).

I tend to agree with this assessment, especially for small to midsize companies. But, I'm acutely aware—having made plenty of mistakes in my own career—that simple organizational answers often don't address the underlying problem you're trying to solve. Over the years, it has become obvious to me that most managers believe changing the people and structure of the organization will have a lot more impact than it actually produces. Organizational changes are very seductive from a management perspective because they are easy to decide upon and quick to implement. They are also very visible, so they show that management is "doing something." In reality, however, it is primarily the underlying culture of the company and its processes that foster increased alignment, not just the organizational structure.

With that said, however, there are five organizational tactics that will improve marketing and sales alignment and effectiveness:

1. The first technique is for management to take a hard look at all of the different organizational entities that support the marketing and sales effort in order to eliminate any duplicate functions and responsibilities. This should include sales operations, field support, product marketing, sales training, and others. This can often be an emotional exercise, but each of these organizations adds some additional infrastructure and expense to the total cost of marketing and sales.

2. The second technique is to actively cross-pollinate the marketing and sales organizations by moving salespeople into marketing and vice versa. As I mentioned in the Introduction, when I was 25 and the top salesperson for a small computer time-sharing company, I was promoted to the position of Marketing Director for an 18-month tour of duty at corporate headquarters. Even though this move resulted in a significant drop in my short-term income, I'm convinced that this has paid for itself many times over. I have also seen several instances throughout my career where marketing people were transferred into a sales support or sales operations role for a time period to round out their skill sets and make them more valuable marketing professionals in the process.

3. The third technique is to disperse the marketing organization geographically to the sales offices so they are closer to the day-to-day selling activities. This geographical alignment allows marketing people to create more localized lead-generation programs and enables them to more closely collaborate with salespeople on the type of selling tools needed to accelerate the customer's buying process.

4. The fourth tactic is to encourage marketing people to go on sales calls to get a better feel for what the salesperson actually goes through. Several years ago, I was visiting a very successful enterprise software company. In a couple of meetings with their marketing team, I heard people refer to a practice they called "NIHITO." I assumed that since this company had a passion for quality, NIHITO must be some form of Six Sigma or quality

management practice that they had learned from the Japanese. When I asked someone to explain it to me, he simply said, "Nothing Important Happens In The Office." In other words, they recognized they learned the most and were most productive when they were out talking to customers. I also learned a great tip from Rob McGovern, a friend of mine who was also the founder and CEO of CareerBuilder.com. He said that when he wanted to know whether his salespeople were delivering the messages correctly, he always went on calls with average performers because he felt that if they got it right, his marketing folks were doing a good job.

5. The fifth organizational technique is to transform sales training from an event-driven organization to an organization that facilitates a continuous learning environment throughout the enterprise. Most salespeople don't want to spend a lot of time in training sessions anyway, and because of the hyper-change happening in most B-to-B markets, the shortening of product and message life cycles, and the amount of turnover in the sales channels, the value of traditional sales training events quickly dissipates.

In today's economy, the sales training organization must:

- Become the evangelist for a more rigorous knowledge-sharing process between marketing and sales, so that the enterprise can capture and leverage market intelligence and best selling practices. As the landmark study by McKinsey called "The War for Talent" concluded, the productivity difference between "A" salespeople and "C" salespeople is as high as 67 percent, and the performance gap between high performers and adequate performers is 40 percent.[2] The new role for sales training is to organize and leverage enterprise knowledge to close these performance gaps in real time.

- Create less stand-alone training content and work closely with the marketing organization to integrate just-in-time e-learning and sales coaching into presentations and other content to deliver knowledge at the point of attack.

- Become more outside-in, moving away from a product-feature focus to a product-usage focus. They must also direct sales training efforts toward gaining a better understanding of the customers' business issues and how they actually use products and services to solve a specific business problem.

- Create performance support systems for salespeople and Internal Champions to ensure they are capable of exploiting the selling tools developed by marketing.

---

[2]"The War for Talent: Organization and Leadership Practice," published by McKinsey & Company, Inc. (New York: 2001).

ALIGNMENT-CENTRIC COMPENSATION
AND RECOGNITION

There are also a few simple compensation and recognition techniques that are helpful in promoting greater alignment between marketing and sales organizations. These techniques should not become significant components of a person's total incentive package, but if implemented correctly, they will increase collaboration and help the Synchronized Marketing and Sales Ecosystem to flourish. They include:

- Providing incentives for marketing professionals that are tied to the growth in the pipeline.
- Putting the marketing team on a bonus program that's tied to the quarterly revenue objectives.
- Giving marketing professionals a quota for days spent in the field.
- Providing a small accelerator to encourage salespeople to forecast accurately and follow up all leads in a timely fashion.
- Publicly recognizing sales and marketing people for actions that demonstrate they are sharing their knowledge regarding what's actually happening in the marketplace, which tactics are working, and which are not.

THE POWER OF PROCESS

The most important thing management can do to enable a Synchronized Marketing and Sales Ecosystem, however, is to embrace process. Integrated processes are what the remaining chapters of *Escaping the Black Hole* are all about.

Most marketing and salespeople are independent by nature, and as such, they often resist process. To counteract this reaction, any new processes need to be simple and non-threatening. Management must find ways to tie the new processes that integrate and align marketing and sales to the broader enterprise objectives of increased customer focus and continuously improving the quality of execution. It is this enterprise-wide commitment to a more customer-centric culture and quality execution that will help get marketing and salespeople on board, thereby enabling management to begin to address the debilitating symptoms of the B-to-B Black Hole.

While the precise amount of integration and alignment from better processes will be difficult to calibrate and quantify in mathematical terms, it will be very easy for employees, partners, prospects, and customers to recognize. Misalignment, just like poor quality, sticks out like a sore thumb, and marketing and sales professionals alike instinctively understand that it makes their jobs and lives more difficult. This makes it easy to get both organizations behind integrated processes that eliminate the waste and frustrations of misalignment while increasing customer focus and improving the quality of the marketing, sales, assets, and activities.

INCREASING MANAGEMENT AWARENESS

What has been really encouraging to me as I was researching the marketing and sales disconnect was the number of managers I encountered who were acutely aware of the problem and who were willing to talk candidly about it. As I discussed in the previous chapter, Mike Bosworth is championing the concept of tighter marketing and sales alignment around a methodology he calls "Customer Centric Selling." And he is not the only one. Insight Technology Group, for example, recently completed its ninth annual survey of more than 220 CRM implementations, and for the third year in a row, the number one priority for these companies was increasing sales and marketing effectiveness. As Jim Dickie who compiled this report says, "Focusing on marketing and sales efficiency is no longer enough for companies. They have come to realize that it is not a matter of having sales reps make more calls. They need to make better calls."[3]

Another one of the catalysts for this increased awareness is the Customer Message Management (CMM) movement. In the spring of 2002, the American Marketing Association held the inaugural forum on a new customer-focused strategy for mapping marketing and sales messaging and communications called Customer Message Management. It was a watershed event where thought leaders including customers, software vendors, industry analysts, and training companies met to grapple with the many substantive issues surrounding marketing and sales alignment, the operational

---

[3]Barry Trailer and Jim Dickie, "Sales Effectiveness Insights: 2004 State of the Marketplace Review," published by CSO Insights.

implications of the business and economic realities of the twenty-first century, and the opportunities and challenges of the new communications environment facing B-to-B companies.

This forum was the first rational and substantive dialogue between software vendors, analysts, and marketing and sales executives on the alignment and effectiveness challenges facing B-to-B organizations. The participants quickly identified the critical need to do a much better job of mapping their messages and improving both the customer centricity and quality of their marketing and sales knowledge and content assets. They also began to define the core principles, technologies, and most of all, processes that would allow companies to systematically leverage their knowledge assets and improve the effectiveness and sales readiness of their marketing and sales content and communications.

Since the inaugural CMM forum, there have been a number of well-attended conferences and Web events sponsored by the AMA, and their Web site contains white papers, best practices, and case studies from a variety of companies, vendors, and consultants who are actively implementing CMM strategies and tactics.

In addition to the CMM movement, other people are beginning to realize the importance of increased alignment between marketing and sales organizations. For example, International Data Corporation (IDC), a leading analyst firm, recently created an industry award called the "Chief Marketing Officer Best Practices Award for Aligning Marketing and Sales." In May of 2004, IDC recognized Siebel Systems, a leading vendor of CRM software and services, with this new award. Siebel won the award by establishing a field marketing organization that deployed staff to sales offices around the globe to collaborate with the local sales teams on creating regional lead-generation programs and pipeline acceleration activities. The results of this initiative were impressive:

- A 100 percent increase in closed opportunities found by marketing
- A 20 percent increase in closed opportunities that were "touched" by marketing programs at some point through the buying process
- A 90 percent increase in sales acceptance of the leads generated by marketing[4]

---

[4]Press release from Siebel Systems (San Mateo, California: March, 2004).

As we will see in later chapters, results like this are not uncommon when you start to make increasing alignment a central theme of your go-to-market strategy, but it does take management vision, focus, and commitment. Unless B-to-B companies begin to address the dysfunction in their marketing and sales organizations in a more systematic fashion and create a more Synchronized Marketing and Sales Ecosystem, the symptoms and statistics referenced at the beginning of this chapter will only get worse. If management is complacent and allows this to happen, the B-to-B Black Hole will get larger and more pervasive until it finally paralyzes the entire organization and ultimately leads to the failure of the business.

CHAPTER 9

Conceptualizing the Ecosystem

IN ORDER TO MAXIMIZE alignment and effectiveness, management needs to view marketing and sales organizations as a single, synchronized ecosystem of continuously improving processes, assets, and activities that enable and facilitate a concentrated focus on the customer. This view enables management to:

- Clearly align the marketing, selling, and buying processes
- Manage the Core Intellectual Assets in a more integrated fashion that maximizes their quality and effectiveness and minimizes their Total Cost
- Coordinate the Critical Communications Activities so that marketing and salespeople speak with a single voice

INTEGRATING AND ALIGNING THE REVENUE PROCESSES

Integrating and aligning the marketing, selling, and buying processes is one of the most important things management can do to create a Synchronized Marketing and Sales Ecosystem.

As Figure 9.1 shows, there are two distinct components of this initiative:

1. Managing the key marketing and selling activities throughout the customer acquisition life cycle—from lead generation through customer satisfaction—as a single, integrated process.
2. Designing this integrated marketing and selling process from the outside-in so that it reflects and is aligned with the way the customer buys products and services.

Integrating and aligning these three fundamental revenue-generation processes in a more systematic fashion will provide significant benefits. A recent study of more than 750 companies by Sales Methodology Experts

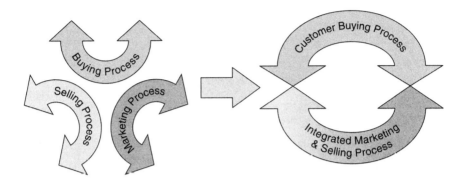

FIGURE 9.1 *INTEGRATING AND ALIGNING THE REVENUE PROCESSES*

showed that just formalizing the sales and marketing process, and managing that integrated process in a systematic fashion, resulted in:

- A 21 percent increase in average order size
- A 21 percent increase in the number of wins
- A 30 percent improvement in forecast accuracy
- A 22 percent reduction in sales cycle time[1]

INTEGRATING THE INTELLECTUAL ASSETS

Establishing a strong foundation for a Synchronized Marketing and Sales Ecosystem requires companies to do a better job of managing the value proposition messages and leveraging the knowledge and best practices scattered throughout the organization. They then need to systematically integrate those knowledge assets with their Sanctioned Marketing and Sales Content to create what I call a 360-degree view of the Core Intellectual Assets (see Figure 9.2). Of all the different factors that drive the ecosystem, this 360-degree view has the most potential to permanently transform the marketing and sales culture, increase long-term effectiveness, and minimize the negative effects of the B-to-B Black Hole.

In order to make this integrated 360-degree view a reality, management needs to implement processes that focus on accomplishing three things:

1. Change marketing and salespeople's thinking from inside-out to outside-in so that they can create Complete Value Propositions. These systematic

---

[1]Dave Roberts, web presentation, hosted by Sales Methodology Experts (Atlanta, Georgia), a division of Siebel Systems, Inc., December, 2003.

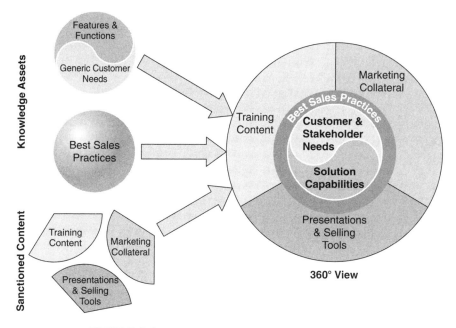

FIGURE 9.2 *INTEGRATING THE INTELLECTUAL ASSETS*

message management processes will enable companies to institutionalize a better understanding of the specific customer problems and stakeholder needs, and how they use the company's products and services to address those needs. This outside-in focus will also help marketing and sales organizations embrace the core principles of solutions-centric selling.

2. Capturing, sharing, and leveraging market intelligence and best sales practices in a systematic fashion.

3. Creating and managing the Sanctioned Content (training content, marketing collateral, presentations, and selling tools) in a way that is consistent with these Complete Value Propositions.

ALIGNING THE CRITICAL COMMUNICATIONS ACTIVITIES

The final aspect of creating a Synchronized Marketing and Sales Ecosystem is the alignment of the Critical Communications Activities that marketing and sales professionals do on a daily basis so they are consistent and coordinated, and they leverage each other (see Figure 9.3). This involves executing these critical activities with a single purpose, a single philosophy, a single vision, and, most of all, a single voice.

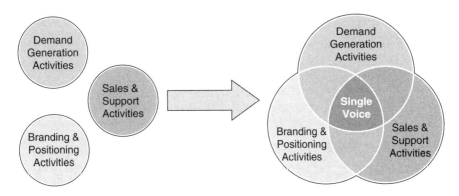

FIGURE 9.3 ALIGNING THE CRITICAL COMMUNICATIONS ACTIVITIES

Since it is the processes and the intellectual assets that drive these Critical Communications Activities, a company's sales and marketing professionals will automatically begin to think alike, act alike, and speak with a single voice when they integrate and align their marketing and sales process and manage their Core Intellectual Assets with a cohesive 360-degree view. The branding and positioning activities will then support the lead-generation activities, and both of these marketing activities will be consistent with the interactions that sales and sales support people have with their prospects and customers each and every day.

THE SYNCHRONIZED MARKETING AND SALES ECOSYSTEM

When the marketing, selling, and buying processes are integrated and aligned, the Core Intellectual Assets are managed in a 360-degree fashion around an outside-in view of the customer. In turn, the Critical Communications Activities are coordinated so that marketing and sales professionals speak with a single voice. Together, this creates a Synchronized Marketing and Sales Ecosystem (as shown in Figure 9.4), in which:

- A deeper understanding of customers' needs and buying processes is institutionalized throughout the enterprise.
- The average salesperson is more productive and requires fewer sales support resources to qualify and close business.
- Marketing activities are more closely tied to revenue.
- The marketing organization is viewed as a vital and indispensable partner in the revenue-generation process.

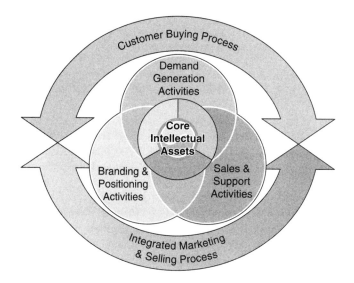

FIGURE 9.4 SYNCHRONIZED MARKETING AND SALES ECOSYSTEM

- Waste is eliminated and costs are controlled, continuously reducing the percentage of marketing and selling expenses to revenue.
- The returns on marketing and sales investments are more measurable.

Aligning these processes, assets, and activities to create this Synchronized Marketing and Sales Ecosystem, however, will require some new, integrated processes that:

- Promote increased alignment and improved execution through the application of systematic and repeatable best practices
- Encourage a more rigorous focus on the customer's real business issues and concerns in both the Core Intellectual Assets and the Critical Communications Activities
- Are reinforced by proven quality-management principles that drive continuous improvement, such as those in well-accepted management systems such as Six Sigma and the Balanced Scorecard

This is why I developed two simple, flexible process models, each containing some new operational tactics that will help managers in all types and sizes of companies create this Synchronized Marketing and Sales Ecosystem. These two models, which are the subject of the remainder of this book, will enable managers to nurture their ecosystems so they will flourish.

CHAPTER 10

Discovering the Holy Grail

I T SHOULD BE OBVIOUS by now that the increasing complexities in the marketplace, coupled with the many different stakeholders involved in a business purchase, demand that B-to-B companies manage their messages in a more systematic fashion. Effective message management is at the heart of a Synchronized Marketing and Sales Ecosystem, and marketing and sales organizations must become more knowledgeable on the specific business problems of the different stakeholders they sell to so they can develop and deliver more Complete Value Propositions.

While this is not rocket science, it does involve synthesizing a lot of different facts, ideas, and insights in a cohesive fashion and then institutionalizing this more complete understanding of all of the customer's needs. If companies can accomplish this, it will enable marketing and sales professionals to more clearly articulate the value and the differentiation of their products and services in their collateral and selling conversations.

All companies attempt to document the different ways they deliver value to the marketplace in some fashion, but few of them go through this process in a systematic way. More often than not, some of the best insights on how to discuss value in the context of specific customer problems and stakeholder needs are never written down. Many of these nuggets of knowledge reside only in the minds of the most experienced marketing, sales, and sales support people. And because these intellectual assets rarely see the light of day, they are not leveraged, often getting lost forever when an expert leaves the company. As a result:

- The institutionalized knowledge of the customers' and stakeholders' needs and issues is superficial at best.
- There is no consistent value vision that extends from the CEO through the salespeople, and most employees struggle with the "elevator speech."
- Value proposition messages are generic and too product-focused, and therefore not as relevant or compelling to the customer as they need to be.

- Companies are unable to adapt to the Shrinking Message Shelf Life phenomenon I described in Part I, and they are slow to react to changes in the marketplace and in the competitive landscape.

- Salespeople are never satisfied with what marketing produces, which is why they constantly ask for new and different pieces of collateral.

- Sales and sales support people spend way too much time and energy changing and creating presentations and customer-facing content.

POSITIONING STATEMENTS AND MESSAGE MAPS

Almost every marketing organization creates some type of positioning statement for their products and services. Unfortunately, these positioning documents are often written in isolation, they usually approach the value proposition from the inside out, and they almost never focus on the specific needs of individual stakeholders. Additionally, in a lot of companies, these positioning statements are never shared with the sales team, so there is minimal feedback and vetting of the value propositions to ensure they are as sales-ready as they need to be. Thus, the collateral and presentations created from these positioning statements reflect neither the market realities experienced by salespeople on a day-to-day basis, nor the way salespeople are actually selling the products and services.

Some companies, however, are beginning to take the positioning process down to the next level by creating what they call "message maps." These message maps are documents that contain more granular value messages and second-level positioning statements organized by vertical industry and, in a few cases, by individual stakeholder. I found that some of the marketing organizations that are building these message maps are doing it in collaboration with their sales teams. Because of this give-and-take process, the resulting value propositions are usually more customer-relevant and complete.

The message-mapping process is an excellent way to initiate more substantive interactions and increase the alignment between marketing and sales professionals. But the more I looked at the actual message map documents that companies were creating, and how sales and marketing professionals were actually using those documents, the more I realized that these message maps were only scratching the surface. And I am not the only person who feels this way. A 2004 study by the CMO Forum of more than 100 chief marketing officers, most of whom had formalized some kind of message-mapping process, concluded, "The consensus of many of our CMO interviewees was that even though they have made major investments in improving messaging over the last year, they still didn't get it right, and that more work was in store in the coming year to develop a compelling message map and content delivery platform."[1]

As I looked harder at how companies were managing their messages, I was able to identify several issues:

- The concept of messaging is inherently inside-out because it focuses on "what I say to whom" instead of what I need to understand. More often than not, people devote too much time and energy to developing the precise words of the message before they have formally agreed upon the precise needs of the customer.

- Most of the message maps I looked at were static documents, and there were no formal processes to continually improve them and keep them updated. As a result, they were ineffective in dealing with the Shrinking Message Shelf Life phenomenon.

- Almost all of the message maps I encountered were superficial and few of them documented the specific needs and issues of the different customer stakeholders and constituencies.

- Because the message maps were created as stand-alone documents, there wasn't any process to connect them to the actual Sanctioned Content created by marketing and used by salespeople on a daily basis.

- Finally, since these message maps weren't shared or leveraged effectively, some of the great insights and ideas discussed during the message-mapping process were never institutionalized and never became part of the fabric of the entire organization.

THE BREAKTHROUGH IDEAS

The more I talked to marketing and sales executives about the increasing complexities of value propositions and some of the inefficiencies and limitations of document-based message maps, the more I started to wonder if a more structured methodology and some basic automation could be applied to the problem in order to:

- Simplify and improve the message development and mapping process so that it would result in more Complete Value Propositions

---

[1]Bill Glazier, "Making Marketing Messaging Meaningful," published by the CMO Council (Palo Alto, California: June 3, 2004).

- Better leverage the facts, opinions, and insights coming out of that process in order to institutionalize a deeper understanding of the customer and stakeholder needs and reinforce principles of solution-centric selling
- Improve the quality and effectiveness of the Sanctioned Content while reducing its Total Cost

As I was thinking through these issues, three ideas kept ringing in my head:

- Why not manage the Core Intellectual Assets like manufacturing organizations manage their raw materials and finished goods inventories?
- Why not use visualization technology to actually map the different elements of a company's value propositions just like geneticists map the human genome?
- Why not enhance the message map with just-in-time sales coaching?

If you could figure out a simple way to accomplish these three things, I thought to myself, it would be like finding the Holy Grail of marketing and sales alignment and effectiveness! First, it would allow companies to create the 360-degree view of the Core Intellectual Assets that becomes the heart of the Synchronized Marketing and Sales Ecosystem I have described. Second, if you were able to graphically represent all the different ways a company's products and services delivered value, and deliver best-sales practices in the context of that model, it would be a whole lot easier to institutionalize a deeper understanding of the customer needs and foster the value-centric culture that would enable that ecosystem to thrive and flourish.

This is why I developed Value Mapping™—a Web-enabled message development and delivery methodology that is based on a patent I was granted back in the late 1990s. Value Mapping uses a few simple question-and-answer templates to help product managers and subject matter experts collaborate and create more Complete Value Propositions for all of the different stakeholders and constituencies that a company's solutions benefit.

Once the Q and A templates are filled out, the answers are then fed into a database that:

- Provides just-in-time coaching to salespeople based upon the precise sales situation they are in
- Creates a customer-centric taxonomy that improves the quality of and simplifies the access to Sanctioned Content

- Graphically maps the Value DNA so the Complete Value Propositions are easier to understand and become institutionalized throughout marketing and sales

APPLYING THE MANUFACTURING MODEL

By viewing the Core Intellectual Assets the same way that manufacturing views inventory, it becomes clear, as shown in Figure 10.1, that these assets are made up of raw materials (facts, opinions, and insights in their most basic form) as well as finished goods (the three different types of Sanctioned Content built to communicate those facts, opinions, and insights).

As Figure 10.1 shows, the knowledge elements (facts, opinions, and insights) that make up the raw materials include:

- The different knowledge elements (Value DNA) that make up the value messages that companies want to convey to the marketplace about how their products and services solve specific customer business problems and stakeholder needs
- The sales intelligence and best sales practices to deliver those messages and accelerate the revenue-generation process

Companies have traditionally focused only on managing the finished goods Sanctioned Content, but until now, no one has ever figured out a simple way to collect, organize, and manage the raw materials knowledge in

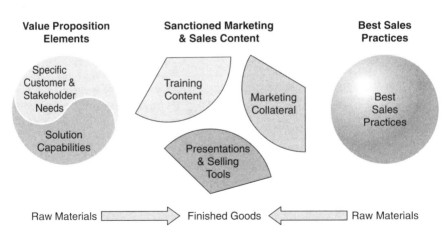

FIGURE 10.1 THE MANUFACTURING MODEL FOR INTELLECTUAL ASSETS

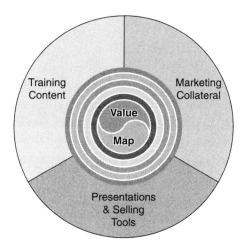

FIGURE 10.2 INTEGRATED KNOWLEDGE AND CONTENT REPOSITORY

a systematic fashion. As a result, marketing and sales organizations never had a way to manage these assets like the proven model that has worked so well for manufacturing organizations.

The Value-Mapping Process solves this problem by creating a Smart Taxonomy that electronically links the raw materials knowledge to the Sanctioned Content, thereby creating an Integrated Knowledge and Content Repository. As Figure 10.2 indicates, this integrated repository creates a single, 360-degree view of all the Core Intellectual Assets so they can be managed in a more cohesive, rational, and efficient manner.

MAPPING THE VALUE DNA

Mapping the human genome helped geneticists improve their knowledge and understanding of the complexities of the human body. This same thinking and strategy can be applied to the concept of Complete Value Propositions. If you were somehow able to systematically catalogue all the different ways a company's solutions delivered value, you could use standard visualization software to map that Value DNA and generate graphical Value Maps. For the first time, these maps would provide marketing and sales organizations with a visual view of the actual value their products and services deliver to different stakeholders. This would make the Complete Value

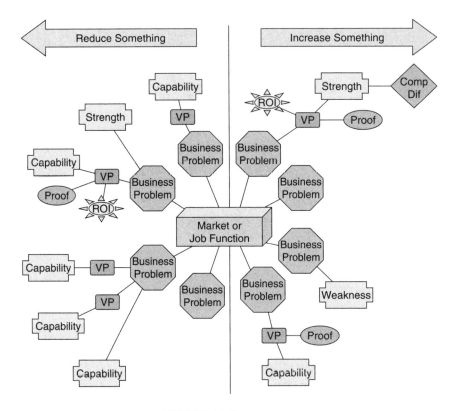

FIGURE 10.3 *VALUE MAP*

Propositions come alive and it would help institutionalize a clearer understanding of that value throughout the organization. The example in Figure 10.3 is just one of the many different views of value that could be generated from this simple database. As you can see, this Value Map breaks down value from the two perspectives that cause customers to buy something:

- The need to reduce something—costs, time, effort, or risk
- The need to increase something, such as revenue, quality, productivity, or competitive advantage

A Value Map would link together various icons to represent the logical relationships between different elements of a Complete Value Proposition:

- The targeted market or job function that has the problems and needs
- The business problems that are of concern to that target market or job function

- The different capabilities, including strengths and weaknesses of a company's solutions
- Techniques on how to differentiate those capabilities
- A description of how value is generated by the capability
- Proof and validation of the value proposition
- Return on investment scenarios

Clicking on an icon on the Value Map (Figure 10.3) would display the underlying knowledge from the database that succinctly and objectively describes that specific element of the value proposition and provides situation-specific coaching to salespeople.

As you can see, this Value Map identifies the various business problems that are potentially important to a specific market or job function. It also identifies which capabilities of a company's solutions address those problems; which of those capabilities are strengths and weaknesses; and which have formal value propositions, proof statements, and ROI scenarios developed for them, and which do not. This Value Map also shows the business problems that the company's solutions do not address.

Value Maps are the only way for companies to automate the message development and mapping process and visualize the value they provide. A picture is worth a thousand words, and Value Maps will go a long way in institutionalizing a better understanding of the customer's needs and creating a strong foundation for a more value-centric culture. These Value Maps will also help marketing professionals more clearly identify what kind of Sanctioned Content is really needed and provide a fact-based framework for the product-planning process.

THE VALUE-MAPPING PROCESS

Value Maps are built through a closed-loop collaborative process (see Figure 10.4) where marketing and sales professionals use simple fill-in-the-blank, Q and A templates to document and continuously improve the key facts, opinions, and insights that make up as many of a company's Complete Value Propositions as possible. These templates can also contain insights on the best marketing and selling practices to deliver and communicate those messages. The Value Mapping templates force a company's subject matter

FIGURE 10.4 *THE VALUE MAPPING™ PROCESS*

experts to provide short, succinct, and objective answers to some key questions regarding the actual value of their products and services. These "Best Answers" identify:

- The key issues surrounding the different business problems of their prospects and customers, as well as the different pains and needs of the different stakeholders their salespeople sell to
- How their customers actually use the capabilities of their products and services to solve those specific issues and pains in a way that more clearly differentiates them from the competition

- Some of the most important knowledge and best sales practices that drive the solutions-selling process, including how to develop needs and qualify prospects, as well as how to quantify, validate, and prove value

These short, succinct Best Answers are automatically fed into a knowledge base that can represent the logical relationships between all of the elements of a Complete Value Proposition. The end result is a continuously improving raw materials inventory of knowledge that connects the dots between problem, solution, and value so that it's easy for everybody in the enterprise to understand. The Value-Mapping Process moves marketing and sales professionals from a superficial to a substantial understanding of their customers' specific business problems. It also can dynamically generate a type of sales "Cliff's Notes," providing salespeople with just-in-time coaching in the context of the specific stakeholder and marketing and sales situation so they can have more relevant and substantive conversations with prospects and customers.

The "Cliff's Notes" analogy is somewhat apt in that they are traditionally created after a book has been written in order to synthesize the essence of that book so it is more easily understood and remembered. Value Mapping represents the Cliff's Notes model in reverse, because the key facts, opinions, and insights that make up Complete Value Propositions are documented and systematically managed in a central place before the Sanctioned Content is written. The Value Map becomes the raw materials that drive the finished goods content as well as all other marketing and sales activities.

I believe that Value Mapping has the potential to become the Holy Grail for marketing and sales alignment and effectiveness because:

- The process is universal and supports all solutions-centric selling methodologies. The input forms are generic, so they are much simpler than most of the forms from sales training companies who are trying to reinforce their specific questioning and communication model.

- Value Mapping will encourage the adoption of solution-centric selling principles by both the sales and marketing organizations, making the content that supports the branding, lead-generation, and selling process more customer- and solution-centric.

- Value Mapping forces marketing and sales professionals to focus more attention on their customers' business issues and needs, and to develop their messages from the outside in. The Smart Taxonomy reinforces a customer- and value-centric culture every time someone accesses a piece of Sanctioned Content. This process helps institutionalize a more detailed understanding of each customer's pains and stakeholder's issues throughout the enterprise.

- Value Maps get everybody from the CEO to the salesperson on the same page, as they are the raw materials that drive all marketing and sales content and communication initiatives. As Tim Riesterer of The CMM Group puts it, "A Value Map is the enterprise compass that always points True North. They bring increased customer focus to the marketing organization and make solution-centric selling come alive for salespeople."

- Value Mapping makes the channels more confident in the value of their products and services. This will empower them to be more aggressive and proactive in calling on the executives in their prospects and customers. This increased confidence alone can have a dramatic effect on the number of calls made and the overall revenue performance.

- Value Mapping helps marketing professionals create better content and manage that content more effectively. It reduces the overall amount of content that's ultimately created by forcing content developers to ask a very important question: "Do I really need a new piece of content, or can I just add another element to the Value Map?"

- Finally, Value Mapping is a simple, scalable process built around a continuous improvement workflow. Product managers can create a basic Value Map in a matter of hours, which they can then enhance and extend over time. In a way, this process is very similar to the way physical maps have developed over the centuries. The first maps created by early explorers were often crude, but as more people used them, the better they became. And the same is true for Value Maps. The continuous improvement workflow built into the process ensures that the value propositions will get harder and more complete as more people use the Value Map.

VALIDATING THE ARCHITECTURE

The more I thought about the concept of an Integrated Knowledge and Content Repository built around a Value Map, the more it became apparent that this two-tier information paradigm fits into the exact same architectural construct that has worked so well for all other enterprise information strategies. That proven model integrates key business processes and larger data stores around a central data asset that is aggressively managed to

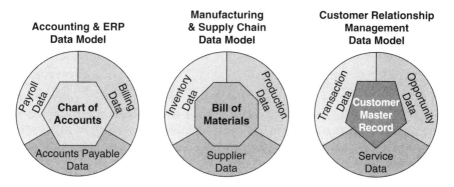

FIGURE 10.5 *PROVEN INFORMATION ARCHITECTURE*

eliminate duplication and maximize accuracy, consistency, and leveragability. As Figure 10.5 shows:

- In Accounting and ERP systems, this central data asset is the central chart of accounts.
- In Manufacturing and Supply Chain systems, this central data asset is the company's bill of materials.
- Finally, in the ideal vision of CRM, this central data asset is the customer master record that enables a single view of the customer.

As you can see, every significant enterprise information strategy is based upon this same two-tier information model. It is efficient, provides maximum leverage, and people understand it. Sure, marketing and sales knowledge and content is unstructured and a lot more fluid than the highly structured data in traditional enterprise information systems, but the model still works.

Unfortunately, the content management community has traditionally approached things from the perspective of a librarian, focusing mainly on the organization and retrieval of the content, not its effectiveness. Because of this librarian-like philosophy, and the technology and infrastructure orientation of the Enterprise Content Management (ECM) vendors, this two-tier information model has not been applied to intellectual assets.

This is why I believe it will be the CRM vendors and marketing and sales consultants, who are much closer to the marketing and sales effectiveness issue, who will become the catalyst for the adoption of the Value-Mapping

Process. As I mentioned in the Introduction, during the mid-1980s I spent some time as the CEO for one of the first commercially available sales automation systems, so I was able to see the CRM market develop firsthand. The sales force automation market limped along for almost ten years before Tom Siebel (the founder and CEO of Siebel Systems) realized that the real business problem companies needed to solve was more than just managing contact information and tracking sales activities. To create a broader enterprise vision and drive the market, he coined the term Customer Relationship Management, and focused his message on the need for companies to eliminate the many silos of customer information they had created, replacing them with a single customer database. Not only would this eliminate the inconsistencies, errors, and duplication of customer information, but it would also enable them to become more customer-centric.

Technical and business people alike intuitively understood the costs and problems of multiple silos, and they quickly embraced the simplicity and common sense of the single customer view concept. The CRM market exploded, and even though it has been a long, tough road, many companies have now eliminated a lot of the duplicate silos of customer information they once had. They are beginning to reach an ideal state where a single customer database drives all of their marketing and sales activities.

I contend that the marketplace for marketing and sales effectiveness solutions is now at the same stage that Customer Relationship Management was in the early 1990s, before that market took off. Companies need breakthrough gains in marketing and sales productivity, the multiple-silo problem surrounding content has reached a crisis stage, and marketing and sales organizations are not nearly as customer- or value-centric as they know they need to be.

This is why Value Mapping may well become the "killer app" for marketing and sales knowledge and content management. It is simple to understand and implement, it helps companies create and harden Complete Value Propositions, it institutionalizes a more customer-centric culture along with the principles of solutions-centric selling, and, finally, it addresses one of the biggest forces driving the Event Horizon of the B-to-B Black Hole by solving the Content Conundrum and lowering the Total Cost of Content.

Just as the single view of the customer from a CRM solution helped companies learn a lot more about their customers and markets, the single view of value found in a well-constructed Value Map will tell executives a lot about where their business is today and where it needs to evolve to tomorrow, both from a strategic and product-planning perspective.

I see a day when Value Mapping becomes as important to the marketing organization as forecasting is to sales. It's a day when product-marketing managers will compete for the mental shelf space of their sales channels by creating better Value Maps, instead of through merchandising gimmicks like newsletters, t-shirts, and coffee mugs. As I write this book, there are only a few small marketing and sales effectiveness software companies who are beginning to adopt some basic Value Mapping concepts and techniques. But because of the many benefits, and the fact that you really can't create a customer-centric marketing and sales environment without one, I predict that more of these vendors will incorporate some kind of Value Mapping functionality into their products.

In the meantime, I let companies license my Value Mapping patent for internal use only, and I only charge a token licensing fee. Additionally, my web site (http://www.web2one.com) includes a current list of software vendors who support the Value-Mapping Process, plus examples of the forms and templates that will enable you to begin building a basic Value Map for your company's products and services.

CHAPTER 11

Enabling the Ecosystem

S O, HOW DO YOU CREATE this Synchronized Marketing and Sales Ecosystem?

As discussed in the last several chapters, creating this ecosystem requires an environment where the daily activities of branding, positioning, lead generation, and sales calls are all executed with a single vision, philosophy, purpose, and, most importantly, a single voice. During my research for *Escaping the Black Hole,* I uncovered several innovative tactics and techniques that companies were implementing to improve alignment, but in most cases, these were stand-alone initiatives, not part of some larger strategic plan to transform the business.

THE NEW PROCESS MODELS

In order to provide marketing and sales executives with a simple way to increase customer focus, communicate the vision of a Synchronized Marketing and Sales Ecosystem, identify the key best practices that will facilitate that ecosystem, and create a framework that will foster increased alignment and effectiveness in the day-to-day marketing and sales activities, I developed two new process models:

1. The Buyer-Centric Revenue Model (BCRM), built around a best practice called Process Synchronization that integrates the marketing and selling activities throughout all the stages of the marketing and sales funnel. It is designed to reduce the friction between those stages and the time to revenue by aligning the marketing and selling process with the way customers purchase complex products and services.

2. The Value-Centric Communications Model (VCCM), which enables companies to implement a CMM strategy, and is built around the Value-Mapping Process described in the last chapter. The VCCM includes several

best practices that continuously improve the customer-centricity, quality, and impact of the knowledge and content assets, and more tightly align those assets with the day-to-day marketing and selling activities.

The ultimate objective of both the BCRM and the VCCM is to improve marketing and sales effectiveness by creating tighter alignment around the customer. This is accomplished by consistently forcing an outside-in perspective so that marketing and sales professionals actually walk the customer-centric walk and continuously improve the quality and effectiveness of the things they produce and the activities they perform each and every day.

Organizational and cultural transformation requires a clear vision, as well as a detailed road map to simplify things for employees and point them in the right direction. I have found the most effective way to accomplish this is through visual process models that enable management to both articulate the broader strategic vision and identify the tactical best practices that make that vision a reality. These visual metaphors often stimulate creativity while getting marketing and sales professionals to keep their eyes on the ball in what often is a chaotic environment. The two new visual models that I developed for the BCRM and VCCM are shown in Figure 11.1.

The result is a pair of simple, scalable, and flexible models for managing marketing and sales organizations so that they continuously improve their

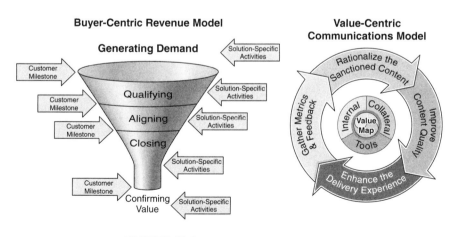

FIGURE 11.1 THE NEW PROCESS MODELS

focus on the customer, their alignment, and their overall effectiveness. These qualities offer several important benefits:

- Simplicity: The primary strength of these two process models is that they are very simple for management as well as employees to understand. This simplicity will allow many of the best practices to be immediately implemented with minimal effort and cost.
- Scalability: Small companies and Fortune 500 enterprises alike can implement each of these process models. The key to this scalability is the fact that the models are all focused on managing the fundamentals more effectively. This focus on the fundamentals applies to any company, no matter what it sells or how big or complicated its direct and indirect channels are.
- Flexibility: Finally, each model is customizable so that companies can pick and choose the specific processes, best practices, and implementation sequence that best fit their current situations. This provides companies with the flexibility to scale their adoption of any part of any model and to implement new processes and best practices at their own pace.

Marketing and sales organizations, by their very nature, need to focus on short-term execution and to react to the chaos and change that the marketplace throws their way every day. These two process models provide a long-term framework that will help them deal with the incessant change they face in a more organized, rational, and creative fashion, and provide them with a structure to efficiently evaluate and implement new best practices. And because these models focus on the fundamentals, they will transcend organizational changes, personalities, and evolving market conditions.

The bad news, of course, is that these new process models, while simple to visualize and understand, require discipline, commitment, and continuous management reinforcement. Even though increased alignment saves lots of time and effort for everybody concerned, the transformation to a Synchronized Marketing and Sales Ecosystem ultimately requires long-term cultural change that can only happen through sustained management commitment and focus.

PART III

IMPLEMENTING THE BUYER-CENTRIC REVENUE MODEL

"Process is the Clark Kent of business ideas, seemingly mild and unassuming, but amazingly powerful . . . it is the discipline that makes outstanding performance a matter of design rather than luck."

—MICHAEL HAMMER IN *THE AGENDA*[1]

---

[1]Michael Hammer, *The Agenda* (New York: Crown Business/Random House, 2001).

CHAPTER 12

Understanding the Model

T wo of the most important aspects of a Synchronized Marketing and Sales Ecosystem that is truly focused on the customer are:

1. A clear, institutionalized understanding of the steps customers go through during their buying processes

2. Integrated marketing and selling activities that leverage each other

As I mentioned in Part I, most of the solutions-centric selling methodologies in the marketplace seem to have been designed from a seller's or inside-out point of view, where the ultimate objective is to manipulate the customer into buying according to the way the methodology teaches salespeople to sell. On top of this, most of the training companies that created these methodologies have not aggressively brought their customers' marketing teams into the loop because the methodology company was more focused on generating the maximum number of sales training days. As result, this parochial and inside-out thinking is often reflected in a company's marketing and sales processes and how those processes get implemented in their CRM system.

Correcting this situation requires two things:

1. Using a technique called Process Synchronization to create a single, integrated marketing and selling process designed around, and aligned with, the way customers actually buy things

2. Managing the key marketing and selling activities in the lead tracking, opportunity management, and pipeline reporting modules of a CRM system as a single, collaborative process

These two objectives are not difficult to achieve if your company sells one product to one market. It can, however, become quite complex for companies that sell multiple products and services to multiple markets. Over the years, I have worked with several single-product start-up companies, as well as large multi-nationals selling lots of different products and services to different markets. I have seen several different approaches to lead tracking, opportunity management, and pipeline reporting during this time, and have made three observations:

1. Few companies have actually integrated their marketing and sales processes.

2. The opportunity management piece is often over-engineered and more complex and onerous than it needs to be. In a lot of companies, the process is so difficult for people to remember that they often get lost in the trees instead of seeing the forest.

3. The sales processes are usually defined from the perspective of a seller's market. As a result, more discipline and rigor is built into the back-end closing activities at the expense of more effective front-end qualification and needs-development practices.

THE LEAKY FUNNEL

While there are different ways to visualize and communicate an integrated marketing and selling process, I believe that the "Leaky Funnel" construct (see Figure 12.1) is the best because everybody intuitively gets it. The potential revenue opportunities from new and existing customers are uncovered through a variety of demand-generation techniques, and they enter through the top of the funnel. Once inside the funnel, they flow through different

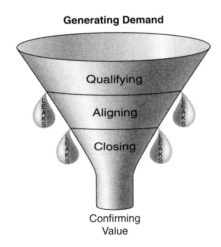

FIGURE 12.1 THE LEAKY FUNNEL

stages. Eventually, they either come out the bottom as paying customers generating new revenue, or they leak out the side of the funnel when it's determined that, for any number of reasons, they are not going to progress any further inside.

One can argue about the number of different stages there actually are in the Leaky Funnel, but over the years I have found it beneficial to use the three internal and two external stages because:

- They cover the whole business acquisition and retention life cycle.
- They are universal and can be applied to any B-to-B company, no matter what their offerings are.
- Management can define clear delineation points and milestones between each stage, which helps them implement more effective pipeline and lead-management processes.

The simplicity and universality of these five stages also makes it easier to adapt to market changes, roll out new products, and integrate acquisitions. But the most important benefit to limiting the funnel to the five stages is that it makes the entire process easy for everyone in marketing and sales to understand and remember, so that this single, integrated process becomes institutionalized, and the marketing and sales disconnect is minimized.

The definitions I use for each of the five stages of the Leaky Funnel are as follows:

1. Demand Generation: This includes both the prospecting done by salespeople and the broad-based communication programs managed by marketing to establish and leverage the brand and produce leads that require channel follow-up. I have always believed that B-to-B branding must be viewed as a demand-generation function, and that the branding programs should be value-centric and designed to generate leads. You can't effectively promote a B-to-B brand without talking about value, and I have yet to see an effective B-to-B branding initiative that didn't also generate some leads.

2. Qualifying: In today's marketplace, qualifying prospects can be extremely difficult and time-consuming. In the 1990s, many sales organizations didn't consider prospects qualified until they had their funding process complete, and they did not invest a lot of resources until that funding was available. Those days are long gone, however, and now companies must invest a lot more resources before the formal funding event. This means

that salespeople have to be able to intelligently discuss business issues with their prospects and customers, and work with them to fully understand, develop, and quantify their needs. The sales organizations that do this well, and more effectively transfer knowledge to their Internal Champions, will have the inside track and a clear, competitive advantage. Qualification occurs when the prospect has developed a vision for solving the problem, made an internal decision to pursue that vision, and both the salesperson and the prospect have agreed, preferably in writing, that they each want to invest in a more detailed and well-defined learning and evaluation process that will eventually require a funding decision for the buyer.

3. Aligning: This is where salespeople learn more specific details about the politics and needs of the different stakeholders who will impact the buying process. It is also the stage in which those stakeholders learn more about the specific capabilities and value that various solutions provide. The goal, of course, is to have buyers and sellers become increasingly aligned around a common vision. It is during this stage that stakeholders develop a detailed vision of a solution, and then start formulating cost projections and budget requests to fund their vision. Internal Champions can be especially valuable during this stage, and marketing organizations need to build content and selling tools to help these Internal Champions perform their cost-benefit analysis and the tasks required by their company's funding process. The Aligning Stage ends at the point where the buyer commits itself to a particular solution, makes a decision to acquire that solution, and formally conveys that decision to the vendor's salesperson in some kind of document.

4. Closing: In many cases, after the decision to buy has been made, the salesperson has to start the education process all over again in order to re-establish the value propositions and negotiate a price that allows the company to maintain its profit margins. The end point of this stage is a signed contract.

5. Value Confirmation: As I mentioned in previous chapters, this stage is becoming more and more critical. It is where the salesperson affirms the buyer's feeling about making a good decision, lays the groundwork for future sales, and uncovers new opportunities. This is also the stage where the salesperson makes the Internal Champions heroes so they become important assets in identifying new revenue opportunities. I believe that the more sales and marketing professionals systematically confirm the value their customers actually realize, the more they learn about their company's value propositions, and the harder and more complete those value propositions become.

ALIGNING THE FUNNEL

There are two major challenges with this Leaky Funnel. As Figure 12.1 demonstrates, it has traditionally been constructed from an inside-out perspective with terminology that reflects what salespeople and marketing people do to customers and prospects, instead of what the customer has to accomplish in order to buy. The other problem is that it does not reflect any anomalies between the way different products and services are sold and bought.

The way to solve both these problems is to visually overlay the seller-centric stages of the Leaky Funnel with solution-specific activities and milestones for both the seller and the buyer in order to synchronize those processes. This Process Synchronization is accomplished by adding two new dimensions to the Leaky Funnel graphic shown in Figure 12.1 to create what I call the Buyer-Centric Revenue Acceleration Model, shown in Figure 12.2.

Using this more advanced model:

- Companies should force themselves to define the key solution-specific buying activities that occur within each stage. This will allow management to map multiple customer buying processes into a single, overall marketing and selling model. Once these solution-specific buying processes have been defined, companies can then define the key marketing and sales

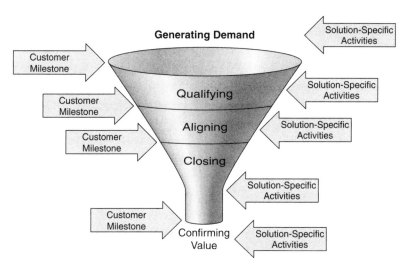

FIGURE 12.2 BUYER-CENTRIC REVENUE ACCELERATION MODEL

activities that will reduce the friction in the customer's buying process so that the speed of the decision making is accelerated. This approach is invaluable for companies who sell different products and services to multiple markets, each with their own specific buying activities and idiosyncrasies. Most of the companies I have worked with on this initially felt there would be considerable process differences between products, services, markets, and product maturity. But in the end, most of those differences were cosmetic in nature, further simplifying the whole definition process.

• At the end of each stage, a specific and easily confirmable customer milestone for each solution is also defined that serves as a formal checkpoint. This confirms that the customer has moved ahead in its buying process, regardless of which product or service is being bought.

While the customer's buying process is always front and center in the Buyer-Centric Revenue Model, it is ultimately designed from both the seller's and buyer's perspective, hence the term Process Synchronization. It reflects both the natural inside-out tendencies of marketing and sales professionals, as well as the outside-in perspective we want to engender in their thinking. Process Synchronization will help marketing create more buyer-centric selling tools that will help their salespeople and Internal Champions reduce friction between the different stages and accelerate the whole process.

Finally, the ability to overlay solution-specific customer buying templates on top of a simple, universal, and integrated marketing and selling process can easily be implemented in most CRM vendors' opportunity and pipeline management modules. This reinforces the customer focus of the BCRM and simplifies its adoption throughout both the marketing and sales organizations.

CHAPTER 13

Integrated Pipeline Management

ONE OF THE MOST IMPORTANT ASPECTS of implementing an integrated and aligned marketing, selling, and buying process is its governance. Even though the Buyer-Centric Revenue Model is relatively simple to understand, I firmly believe this integrated process must be managed as a living, breathing entity with rigorous reporting systems so that aggressive lead management and pipeline management become ingrained in the sales and marketing culture.

One of the most interesting things I discovered in my discussions with marketing and sales executives over the last several years was how little most of them understood about what was actually happening with their leads and pipelines. While some of them had implemented rudimentary lead management and opportunity management processes as part of their CRM initiatives, almost every company was still arguing over the quality of leads and spending a considerable amount of time and effort trying to forecast accurately, usually with less than stellar results. As I drilled in deeper on the problem, I discovered that in almost every company the lead tracking system was different than the opportunity management system, and the forecast system didn't tie into either. In other words, they had created multiple information systems and silos with duplicate, erroneous, and often conflicting information. Additionally, I found very few companies making any substantive efforts to track the changes in their pipeline over time in order to better understand some of the underlying dynamics affecting their markets.

I have long believed that a more holistic and systematic approach to managing the entire customer and revenue acquisition process as a single pipeline offers an enormous opportunity for marketing and sales management. It allows companies to better understand their business while aligning their marketing and sales organizations. There are three fundamental principles to this integrated approach to pipeline management:

1. Leads, opportunities, and forecasts should be managed in a single information system that mirrors the top four stages of the Buyer-Centric Revenue Model from demand generation through closing the sale. This single integrated system should automatically generate the starting point for the bottom-up forecast (which is an entirely different discipline than pipeline management), and it should provide multiple views of the pipeline:

    a. Sales views, which show pipeline information from an organizational perspective (salesperson, district, region, channel, etc.)

    b. Marketing views, which show the same information from either a product or program perspective

2. B-to-B pipelines are like living organisms that change their shape and internal behavior over time. Even small changes in a pipeline are often early indicators of evolving market dynamics as well as potential organizational and employee problems. By collecting a few simple metrics from this integrated lead disbursement/opportunity management system, and tracking these metrics on a monthly basis, it's easy to run time-series analyses and create graphs that show how the key aspects of lead generation, lead follow-up, and sales cycles are evolving. I have become a big believer in these time-series analytics because they are easy to implement, they visually show the changes happening in all views of the pipeline, and they provide feedback and early warnings to salespeople as well as management of things that need to be addressed.

3. The lead and opportunity management system should be kept simple for salespeople. Throughout my career, I have seen sales processes that were over-engineered with too many steps, detailed follow-up forms for each lead, and comprehensive input and change management forms for every opportunity. Invariably, this rigidity doesn't reflect the actual fluidity and chaotic nature of the B-to-B selling and buying process. It results in a lot of work and often creates a threatening environment for salespeople. I can't recall a single situation in which a complex sales process and opportunity management system was really being used by the salespeople or generating reliable management information. As I mentioned in the previous chapter, I believe that the opportunity management process should be based on as few steps as possible, the lead follow-up process should be accomplished with just a few clicks, and inputting and updating an opportunity record should be designed to

require no more than two to three minutes each month. To achieve this, the data collection system should include as many checklists as possible to minimize keystrokes, and it should only ask for the basic demographics of an opportunity that will be regularly measured and reported on.

During the last seven years, I have encountered a few companies that were beginning to implement two new integrated pipeline management processes that seem to have a lot of potential. Together, these new processes will improve lead quality and enable marketing and sales organizations to more effectively share operational information, increase their alignment, and better understand their business.

These two new integrated pipeline management processes are:

1. A more collaborative and integrated lead tracking and management process that focuses on improving the quality of leads and more rationally assessing their total impact throughout the entire marketing and sales funnel.

2. A method for tracking the changes in pipeline behavior through a technique I call Pipeline Radar™ that systematically records and reports on the key behavioral attributes of a pipeline over time, much like conventional radar records and tracks the movement of an airplane.

These new integrated pipeline management processes can significantly improve the operational information for management as well as employees, and they can provide some extraordinary insights into what's actually happening during the selling process. They also encourage more collaboration between marketing and sales professionals and give each organization more insight into some of the issues and challenges faced by the other. This goes a long way toward improving communication, breaking down barriers, and minimizing some of the dysfunction that drives the growth of the B-to-B Black Hole.

INTEGRATED LEAD MANAGEMENT

As the research I cited in Part I indicates, after the conflicts and disconnects over the development and delivery of the value proposition messages, the leads generated by marketing are the most contentious issue between B-to-B marketing and sales organizations. The three flashpoints that ignite this issue are lead quality, lead follow-up (several studies have shown that as much as 80 percent of the leads generated by marketing activities never get followed up by salespeople[1]), and the failure to give the marketing organization credit when credit is due.

While there is no way to fully eliminate these arguments, they can be mitigated through three simple best practices that create a more collaborative, integrated, and rational approach to demand generation and lead tracking:

1. Formally defining and segmenting leads
2. Getting sales to provide basic feedback on every lead
3. Capturing and publishing more robust lead tracking and contribution statistics

DEFINING AND SEGMENTING LEADS   No two leads are alike, and because of this and a host of other cultural and historical factors, most sales and marketing professionals have developed completely different views of what a lead should be. Until the two organizations agree on a common definition of a lead, along with the specific criteria for assessing lead quality, this issue will always get in the way of improving alignment and effectiveness. So, marketing and sales organizations must first formally define what a lead actually is in the context of their specific business model and go-to-market strategy.

For coming up with a common definition that will make both organizations happy, I have found three techniques that seem to produce quality results. They are:

1. Viewing leads as information, not as potential revenue. First of all, this takes a lot of the emotion and ambiguity out of the definition process. By focusing on the information content of leads, it allows people to rationally discuss the different kinds of information that increase a lead's quality and value. It also serves as a template to more rationally factor lead information into a more practical and repeatable assessment of lead quality that considers more than whether or not a sale was ultimately closed and for how much. B-to-B sales opportunities evolve over time as more and more information and knowledge is gathered. The lead represents the beginning

---

[1]Sheryl Kingstone, "Improving Sales Effectiveness in a Down Economy," Blueprint Marketing, Yankee Group (Boston, Massachusetts: 2002): 10.

of that information-gathering process. As such, the value of the lead should be assessed at that time because so much of the eventual information is collected through activities that are out of marketing's control, after the lead is passed along to a salesperson.

2. Segmenting and grading leads based upon the level of information. For example, sales and marketing could jointly define three types of leads as follows, each type having a greater value than the type before. Marketing would then structure the lead disbursement process to reflect these classifications:

   a. Type One: Contains contact information and how the lead was generated

   b. Type Two: Contains type one information plus specific information on the pain or business issue the prospect is experiencing, along with other predefined sales information, such as whether or not a budget exists

   c. Type Three: Contains type two information plus a scheduled follow-up sales event, such as a sales call, phone call, or Web meeting

3. Recognizing that demand-generation activities have two key objectives: The first and most obvious objective of demand-generation programs is to uncover new opportunities. The second is to accelerate existing opportunities in the sales pipeline by generating additional contacts on the buyer's team and reinforcing the selling message. I have seen many instances in which an important new contact in an existing opportunity was uncovered by a marketing activity. This sales cycle reinforcement component of marketing programs often goes unnoticed and unappreciated, so it needs to be measured and recognized.

CAPTURING FEEDBACK FROM SALES Once marketing and sales have agreed upon a common definition, and the marketing organization is classifying all leads according to that definition, it is critical for the sales organization to commit to providing basic feedback on every lead. This feedback process should be an integrated part of the lead-dissemination and opportunity-management processes, and it should require as little effort and thinking on the part of the salesperson as possible. In working with one of my clients on this lead-feedback process, we came up with a simple automated checklist that became part of the actual lead record that takes two to three minutes for salespeople to complete. The lead distribution and opportunity management system requires the salesperson to fill out this checklist for every lead, regardless of the lead type. It is so simple that the salespeople agreed to fill it out immediately after making initial contact with the lead.

The checklist indicates several key pieces of information:

- Contact was made? "Yes" or "No"
  - If "No" was checked
    - Tried but failed.
    - Did not try (it was OK for the salesperson to check this box because there are many good reasons for not following up, but we wanted them to formally acknowledge making that decision).
  - If "Yes" was checked, the sales rep was asked to check whether or not additional action was planned? (Checking "No" automatically removed the lead from the salesperson's database)
- If "Yes" was checked, other checkboxes followed:
  - New opportunity?
    - Checking this box forced the lead to be formally placed in the salesperson's opportunity management system.
  - Existing opportunity?
    - Which one? (Checking this brought up a pick list from the opportunity management system of the existing deals in this salesperson's pipeline.)

This simple checklist enabled the marketing organization to measure:

- How long it took for sales to follow up (all dates were automatically captured by the system).
- Whether or not the salesperson considered the lead to be of value (it was valuable if they checked the additional action box).
- Where the marketing activity contributed in the sales process (new or existing).

Also, by tying the lead to an existing opportunity in the opportunity management system, the marketing organization was able to measure all of the potential as well as actual revenue they touched with their lead programs.

PUBLISHING THE LEAD METRICS The third best practice for a more integrated and robust lead-management process is to collect and publish key demand-generation metrics on a company-wide basis so they are visible to the entire enterprise. This reinforces the total value of the marketing efforts, and shows how well the measurement process is actually working. These should include:

- Metrics on the total volume of leads passed to sales by type
- Metrics on actual sales follow-up, including the delay factor
- Metrics on leads where sales felt they were good enough to warrant additional activity
- Metrics on whether the leads were for new or existing opportunities
- Close ratios and revenues associated with all the leads marketing touched, whether they were new or existing opportunities

AGGRESSIVELY MANAGING THE PIPELINE

In addition to a more holistic and integrated approach to lead management, there is another new pipeline management process some companies are beginning to experiment with that I call Pipeline Radar™. I believe it will significantly improve the accuracy of forecasting while:

- Helping to align marketing and sales organizations on long-term market strategies and tactics
- Providing the marketing and salespeople some additional insights on what they could do to improve their individual performance

Pipeline Radar makes use of the new analytic capabilities that are being offered by most CRM systems. These capabilities systematically measure and graphically report on key pipeline behavior attributes and how these attributes are changing over time. It creates a much higher visibility of the pipeline throughout marketing and sales organizations; allows people to use triangulation techniques to spot significant market, operational, and performance trends earlier; and provides additional information to management for increasing the accuracy of the forecasting process.

There are several reasons why it is more important than ever to systematically track pipeline behavior:

- As I mentioned earlier, B-to-B pipelines are like living organisms, constantly evolving and changing. As such, they are the best leading indicators of the long-term health of the marketplace and the business, as well as the effectiveness of sales personnel and marketing programs. Because of the complexity and chaos of the B-to-B marketing, selling, and buying processes, it is important to look for pipeline behavior patterns that foreshadow significant changes in the marketplace or provide early indications of potential strategy, execution, or employee performance problems. By more systematically tracking and graphing pipeline behavior metrics for both the sales view (salesperson, geographic organization, channel organization) and the marketing view (product, program), it simplifies things for both employees and managers. This simplification enables them to ask better questions sooner about trends and behaviors that would normally go unnoticed, and to take early action to avoid serious problems.

- B-to-B pipelines are made up of opinions and conjecture as well as facts. They often contain significant erroneous and misleading information, which often creates what I call "artificial pipeline inflation and deflation." Some of this artificiality is a natural occurrence driven by a combination of the varying (conservative vs. optimistic) personalities of the salespeople and their managers, plus a natural aversion to sharing information and being managed on the part of salespeople.

    The current business environment also increases the amount of artificiality in the pipeline. In good economic times, pipelines and forecasts tend to be on the conservative side, but in a challenging business climate like what we have now, they tend to be overly optimistic. In this economy, artificial pipeline and forecast inflation has become a serious problem for many companies, especially those with complex sales cycles. Joe Galvin, Vice President of Gartner Group's CRM practice, put this succinctly when he told me: "There's a significant amount of fear in salespeople and sales management right now, and this fear causes a lot of them to conclude that the longer they delay bad news, the better. First of all, they don't want to get beaten up twice, once for a low forecast and again for missing their numbers. Second, because of their nature, they always hope that some miracle will save them."

    Tracking long-term pipeline behavior in a more systematic fashion makes the accuracy of the pipeline a visible issue for the entire enterprise. Over time, this visibility leads to more fact-based pipeline information and, ultimately, more reliable forecasts.

- Implementing a more systematic and visible approach to pipeline management creates two important cultural benefits that improve overall alignment and effectiveness:

    1. It forces the individual sales and marketing people to think longer term, and to spend more time on pipeline development activities.

2. It enables marketing and sales professionals to interact with each other and with management to ask the question, "What is really happening to the pipeline?" Regular discussions on pipeline behavior often lead to new ideas on strategies and program tactics, as well as to clearer definitions of the kind of content and selling tools needed by the channels.

In the early 1990s when I was running the marketing and sales organizations for a five-million-dollar enterprise software company, I had my sales operations staff develop an early version of a pipeline behavior tracking system. Even with the rudimentary technology available back then, we were able to achieve a higher visibility of the pipeline throughout both organizations. We were also able to uncover some significant patterns in pipeline behavior that allowed us to ask more pointed questions about the revenue forecasts, and to triangulate those answers with other information to increase forecast accuracy. Finally, by tracking the behavior of the pipeline, we were able to make more informed decisions about personal, product direction, and marketing programs.

PIPELINE RADAR REPORTING

There are two primary aspects of pipeline behavior that can be easily measured over time so they can be visualized through graphs and charts from a Pipeline Radar system. These two aspects are:

1. External behavior, which includes the attributes of size and shape
2. Internal behavior, which includes the attributes of flow, leakage, and turbulence

There are lots of ways to analyze and visually graph these pipeline behavior attributes, and each company needs to choose a set of external and internal pipeline metrics and graphs that best reflects their marketing and sales process, business model, and culture. As I mentioned earlier, most CRM companies are starting to address analytics in their products and to support some of these concepts, but I have found that sales process specialists such as Market-Partners (http://www.market-partners.com), are leading the way in nailing the problem. Market-Partners has developed a CRM plug-in for managing pipeline behavior called the eSP Toolkit™ that is getting rave reviews from their customers because it finally allows them to see what is actually happening to their pipeline.

For your convenience, I have included a few simple examples of Pipeline Radar reports that can be easily be generated in Microsoft Excel™ from the data that's already captured in a basic opportunity management system. Over the next several years, I expect most CRM vendors will incorporate richer templates and process assists into their products for more advanced forms of Pipeline Radar so that this type of reporting can be more tightly integrated into the opportunity management process.

TRACKING THE PIPELINE'S EXTERNAL SIZE AND SHAPE The most basic pipeline attribute is overall size, including whether it has a confidence factor applied to it or not. Both aspects of every marketing and sales pipeline should be tracked on a regular basis from both a revenue and number of opportunities standpoint. As Figure 13.1 shows, comparing pipelines to a standard benchmark, perhaps a corporate average, can be a powerful way to stimulate substantive discussions with both the sales and marketing professionals.

Tracking how the shape of a pipeline changes over time, both in terms of how much revenue and how many opportunities are at each stage of the

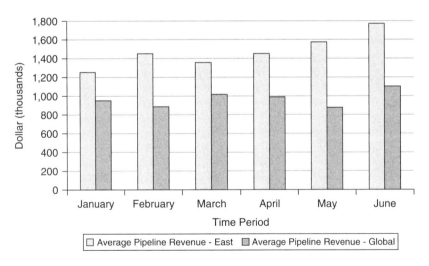

FIGURE 13.1 PIPELINE RADAR SIZE COMPARISON

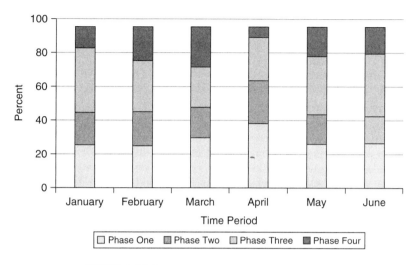

FIGURE 13.2 *PIPELINE RADAR SHAPE ANALYSIS*

funnel, is not as common as tracking overall size. However, tracking the shape of a pipeline (see Figure 13.2) can tell a lot about a salesperson's or sales and marketing organization's ability to generate new interest or cultivate needs in their opportunities. It also reveals where to spend additional time and effort. It's critical, however, to remember that different salespeople work differently, so it is the change in the shape of a pipeline over time that is often more important than the actual shape itself.

TRACKING INTERNAL FLOW AND TURBULENCE Very few companies attempt to track the internal flow of opportunities within a pipeline on a regular basis, but it's extremely simple to do and can provide enormous insights for management, marketing, and sales professionals. Tracking flow involves measuring what new opportunities came into the funnel, what opportunities leaked out the side of the funnel, what opportunities carried forward to subsequent months, which of those opportunities progressed to a new stage, and which opportunities actually closed. As shown in the three charts in Figures 13.3, 13.4, and 13.5, pipeline flow can be measured both in the aggregate with a mathematically calculated "flow factor," or it can be graphed to show how the flow is actually happening and how the pipeline is changing behavior depending on the stage of the funnel.

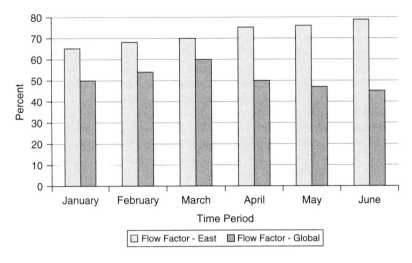

FIGURE 13.3 *PIPELINE RADAR FLOW FACTOR COMPARISON*

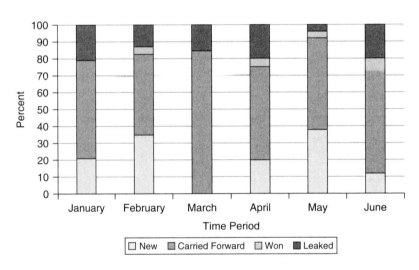

FIGURE 13.4 *PIPELINE RADAR FLOW PROFILE ANALYSIS*

Figure 13.5 shows one of the key pipeline behaviors to measure—"days in stage" because of the significant time, effort, and costs expended on each opportunity. In today's marketplace, it is important to make sure that salespeople do not keep things in the pipeline longer than they should. I know this may sound like heresy, but since a majority of sales are won or lost in

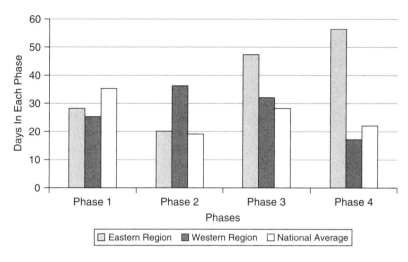

FIGURE 13.5 PIPELINE RADAR-FLOW DAYS IN STAGE COMPARISON

the early stages of the selling process, I believe it's often the best strategy to cut your losses early and expend your valuable sales and marketing resources on deals that have a higher chance of success. As Sam Reese, the President and CEO of Miller Heiman, says in the book entitled *The Sales and Marketing Excellence Challenge:* "In today's market we are deathly afraid of losing deals; we try to do whatever it takes to avoid losing. An interesting question I have been exploring with companies is, 'What is actually the worst thing that can happen when you lose a deal?' When you really consider the problem, you realize that only one bad thing can happen when you lose—which is that it takes you a long time to lose."[2]

TRACKING PIPELINE TURBULENCE The final internal pipeline behavior attribute that's worth measuring and tracking is pipeline turbulence. Pipeline turbulence occurs when an existing opportunity changes somehow as it progresses through the different stages of the sales funnel. The changes in an opportunity involve the size and expected close date, and they can be either negative or positive. Negative turbulence is when deals get smaller

---

[2]Jim Dickie and Barry Trailer, *The Sales and Marketing Excellence Challenge: Changing How the Game Is Played* (Mill Valley, California: Sales Mastery Press, 2003).

(either in actual size or confidence factor) or are delayed, and positive turbulence is when they get larger or are expected to close sooner. It's important to measure turbulence for a lot of reasons, not the least of which is that salespeople who are in trouble often use positive turbulence as a way to artificially inflate their pipeline and obfuscate the issues to avoid or delay a negative performance review. As Figures 13.6 and 13.7 show, just like flow,

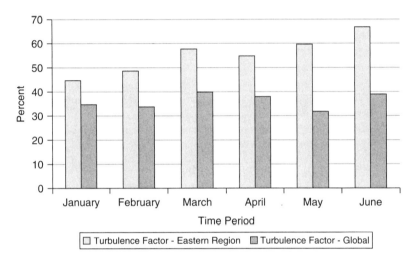

FIGURE 13.6 PIPELINE RADAR TURBULENCE FACTOR COMPARISON

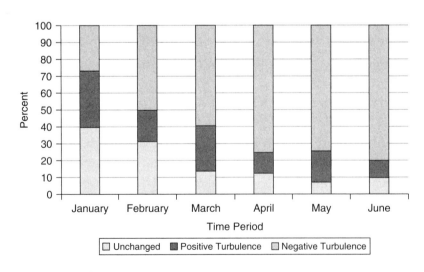

FIGURE 13.7 PIPELINE RADAR TURBULENCE ANALYSIS

turbulence can be measured in the aggregate through a mathematically calculated turbulence factor, or it can be analyzed in terms of the type of turbulence the pipeline is experiencing.

CAPTURING PIPELINE BEHAVIOR DATA The good news about actively measuring pipeline behavior is that it requires no additional input from salespeople. The data is almost always readily available from a standard opportunity management system. For example, capturing just four fields of information on a regular basis, and running an automatic comparison routine to calculate and capture the changes in pipeline structure from month to month, generated all of the examples shown in this chapter. Those four fields are:

1. The current date
2. The size of the opportunity (factored and not)
3. The current stage of the funnel or sales process
4. The expected close date

By taking a snapshot of these four data points on a regular basis and calculating certain changes in key behavior metrics, you will produce a valuable time-series database that makes it simple to measure and track the external and internal behavior, including flow and turbulence, from month to month.

BEST PIPELINE RADAR AND REPORTING PRACTICES There are a couple of best practices that enable B-to-B companies to get the most out of their pipeline management initiatives. These include:

- Capturing pipeline statistics on both dollar volume and the number of active opportunities.
- Creating a system where marketing and salespeople alike can run Pipeline Radar reports for their own territory or product set. This is best accomplished by automatically running a size analysis for every salesperson as part of the pipeline update process, and giving them a pick list of personalized reports they can easily run on demand.
- Publishing overall corporate Pipeline Radar reports on size and shape for everybody in the company to see.

- Developing national benchmarks for sales organizations as well as products and programs for certain pipeline attributes and behaviors to use for comparison.
- Adding two confidence factor fields in the pipeline record, one for close date and one for size. This forces more thinking on the part of salespeople and leads to more accurate forecasts.
- Recording the reason for leaks so you can determine whether opportunities were removed because of competition, ineffective qualification, budgetary limitations, etc.

PART IV

IMPLEMENTING THE VALUE-CENTRIC COMMUNICATIONS MODEL

"In order to be effective, a salesperson must be able to relate his or her offering to the buyer in a way that will allow that buyer to visualize using it to achieve a goal, solve a problem, or satisfy a need. This in turn requires a conversation . . . Sales-Ready Messaging must be created to support targeted conversations with decision makers and decision influencers."

—MICHAEL BOSWORTH AND JOHN HOLLAND IN *CUSTOMERCENTRIC SELLING*[1]

---

[1]Michael Bosworth and John Holland, *CustomerCentric Selling* (New York, New York: McGraw-Hill, 2004).

CHAPTER 14

Understanding the Model

A S WE HAVE SEEN THROUGHOUT this book, the foundation of a Synchronized Marketing and Sales Ecosystem is a more systematic knowledge, content, and communications process that integrates the creation, management, and delivery of the Core Intellectual Assets. This more holistic approach will harden the value propositions and get marketing and sales organizations on the same page so they always speak with one voice. If done well, this integrated process will also reduce the Total Cost of Content, increase revenue production, and build sustainable competitive advantage by transforming the way the marketing and sales organizations interact and operate on a day-to-day basis. I contend, however, that this broader and more comprehensive strategy will only be successful by combining proven quality management principles, systematic processes, and modern computer and communications technologies. The results will be:

- An integrated view of the Core Intellectual Assets that can be managed in a way that increases the consistency of those assets, while reducing the total cost of creating and using those assets
- A continual improvement in the customer-centricity, relevancy, and quality of those intellectual assets, thereby improving their impact on the revenue generation process
- Increasing alignment between the branding strategy, the lead-generation programs, and the day-to-day selling interactions of sales and sales support people

As I mentioned in Part II, the Customer Message Management movement has created a national dialogue on the need for more customer-centric and sales-ready messaging. In my research I was also able to find several companies making some headway on this vision. Most of these companies, however, had never developed a long-term management framework to address message and content management from both a tactical and strategic perspective.

STRATEGIES AND PRINCIPLES

Because of this vacuum, I developed the Value-Centric Communications Model (VCCM). It's a comprehensive and systematic knowledge, content, and communications process for managing and leveraging all of the Core Intellectual Assets of a marketing and sales organization in a more cohesive, integrated, and effective manner. The VCCM provides management with a simple visual to get everybody on board with the long-term vision and strategy as well as the day-to-day activities and objectives. It is based upon four overriding strategies:

1. Redefining the raw message assets as the compilation of the key facts, ideas, and insights that make up Complete Value Propositions, and managing those assets through a Value Map in much the same way a manufacturing organization manages its raw materials inventory.

2. Integrating the Value Map with the Sanctioned Content to create a 360-degree view of the Core Intellectual Assets so that these critical assets can be more effectively managed and leveraged.

3. Continually improving both the customer-centricity and the quality of the Core Intellectual Assets, as well as the way those assets are delivered, so that the knowledge-transfer experience is significantly improved.

4. Aggressively exploiting the Internet as a primary communications platform for both the marketing and sales organizations.

Companies have traditionally approached knowledge and content management primarily from the perspective of a librarian. As such, their focus is on answering the question, "How do I organize and control all this stuff so people can find it?" While organization, administration, access, and control are certainly important aspects of the VCCM, additional emphasis and focus are placed upon continually improving the quality and effectiveness of the assets and maximizing business results.

Another major difference is that traditional content management strategies only focus on managing the Sanctioned (finished goods) Content. The VCCM, on the other hand, is also concerned with managing, leveraging, and exploiting the raw material (facts, opinions, and insights) knowledge that drives the finished product, just as manufacturing organizations manage both their raw materials and finished goods inventories.

	Traditional Content Management	Value-Centric Communications Model
Improve the quality of the underlying knowledge	*No*	*Yes*
Improve the way you communicate information	*No*	*Yes*
Improve how you organize sanctioned content	*Yes*	*Yes*
Improve how you update the content	*Yes*	*Yes*
Improve how people access the content	*Yes*	*Yes*
Improve the understanding and retention of information	*No*	*Yes*
Improve how well the content influences behavior	*No*	*Yes*

FIGURE 14.1 VCCM VS. TRADITIONAL APPROACHES

Some of the key differences between traditional approaches to content management and the Value-Centric Communications Model are shown in Figure 14.1.

The Value-Centric Communications Model is all about process. It borrows many of the lessons learned from the TQM movement and applies them to marketing and sales organizations to create a more customer-centric culture, increase creativity and innovation, and improve execution. The VCCM positively impacts both the top and bottom line by:

- Improving the effectiveness of the branding and lead-generation programs and, as a result, the average quality of the leads
- Increasing the average revenue per sale
- Increasing the close rates and reducing sales cycle time
- Reducing the cost and increasing the effectiveness of sales training
- Reducing the ramp-up time to productivity for salespeople and channels
- Reducing the total cost of sales and sales support
- Reducing the Total Cost of Content, including creation, maintenance, delivery, and usage

THE VCCM ARCHITECTURE

The best way to view the Value-Centric Communications Model is as a closed-loop, continuous improvement process composed of two major components:

1. An Integrated Knowledge and Content Repository
2. A Content Optimization Framework

The VCCM is built upon the concept of an Integrated Knowledge and Content Repository (see Figure 14.2) where the Sanctioned Content is aligned and managed around a Value Map. This two-tier architecture more tightly integrates the raw materials knowledge with the finished goods enabling a 360-degree view of the Core Intellectual Assets that minimizes duplication and redundancies. This architecture reduces the Total Cost of Content while increasing the value and impact of these critical enterprise assets on the revenue-generation process.

The second component of the VCCM is a Content Optimization Framework (see Figure 14.3) that identifies and reinforces the four critical sub-processes needed for more effectively developing, managing, and delivering Sanctioned Content. These sub-processes are:

1. Rationalizing the Sanctioned Content by:
   - Consolidating the content silos to reduce duplication and redundancy

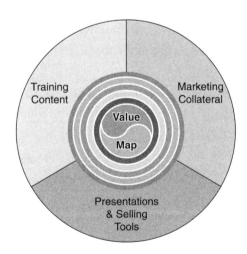

FIGURE 14.2 INTEGRATED KNOWLEDGE AND CONTENT REPOSITORY

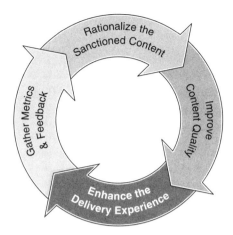

FIGURE 14.3 CONTENT OPTIMIZATION FRAMEWORK

- Restructuring the Sanctioned Content from both a physical and logical perspective to make it more effective
- Reducing the total amount of Sanctioned Content

2. Improving content quality by:
   - Using more templates and proven content-creation techniques that enhance accuracy, precision, clarity, and production value
   - Implementing best practices to ensure that the Sanctioned Content is always current

3. Enhancing the user's delivery experience through:
   - More interactive, personalized, and customizable content for more targeted one-to-one communications
   - The creation of a continuous learning environment where the Sanctioned Content promotes comprehension and retention so it has the maximum impact on the recipient's attitudes and behavior, whether they are a prospect, customer, salesperson, or partner

4. Measuring usage and gathering feedback to:
   - Identify the most productive content and ensure continuous improvement
   - Track who is using the documents, selling tools, and presentations, and which content is most effective in accelerating the marketing, selling, and buying process

By adopting a rigorous Value Mapping process and wrapping the best practices of the Content Optimization Framework around an Integrated

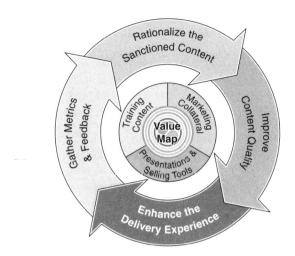

FIGURE 14.4 THE VALUE-CENTRIC CONTENT AND COMMUNICATIONS MODEL

Knowledge and Content Repository, you create the entire Value-Centric Communications Model, as diagrammed in Figure 14.4.

As I mentioned at the beginning of this chapter, implementing the VCCM is a multi-faceted, multi-year, strategic initiative that is the heart and soul of a Synchronized Marketing and Sales Ecosystem. Taking this strategic long-term view will also help marketing and sales professionals adapt to change and embrace the new communication environment of the twenty-first century. It will also encourage them to completely rethink the way they manage their content, coordinate their lead-generation activities, and develop more robust content and tools for the channel so that salespeople can increase the value they provide to customers and prospects.

Finally, it is important to remember that the VCCM is a strategic framework that represents a continually growing management toolbox of marketing and sales effectiveness techniques, tactics, technologies, and tools. As more companies employ some of these techniques, tactics, technologies, and tools, they will undoubtedly discover new and better ways to do things and add them to the toolbox.

CHAPTER 15

Adopting the VCCM

THERE ARE THREE MAIN PHASES to implementing the Value-Centric Communications Model:

1. The first phase is to implement the Value-Mapping Process.

2. The second phase is to do a one-time cleanup of the existing Sanctioned Content to consolidate some of the different content silos and eliminate the duplicate and redundant content.

3. The third phase is to begin adopting some of the processes in the Content Optimization Framework.

GETTING STARTED

There are several best practices that will help companies kick off the implementation of the Value-Centric Communications Model:

- Make this a "C" level issue. In order for the VCCM initiative to get the proper traction, the chief operations, marketing, and sales officers must buy into the long-term vision of a Synchronized Marketing and Sales Ecosystem. There are a couple of things that can be done to get these executives on board:

  - Educate them on the basics. Start talking about the problems caused by misalignment, and promote the idea that the value proposition messages and Sanctioned Content are important enterprise assets. One technique that always seems to work is to get the management team together with a couple of sales and marketing people, and ask each of them to take 10 minutes to write down the essence of the company's primary value proposition. Then compare what they have written down. It is usually very enlightening.

  - Perform an assessment of the current state of affairs, and try to put some hard costs around the actual impact of the B-to-B Black Hole. Every company I know of that has done this type of assessment has been surprised by their actual Total Cost of Content.

  - Tie the VCCM into an existing enterprise management initiative. If your company has made a strategic commitment to a process-based management strategy such as Six Sigma or the Balanced Scorecard, wrap this initiative into that strategy to get marketing and sales on board with the program.

- Begin the Value-Mapping Process. Even if a company never adopts any of the more rigorous processes and best practices of the VCCM, it needs to develop a basic Value Map. Once most "C" level executives see this process in action and begin to understand its impact on the way people think about their customers and their products, these executives will buy into the bigger vision for a comprehensive and systematic approach to developing and managing the message and content assets.

- Appoint a champion. To be successful, any significant enterprise transformation initiative needs a champion to evangelize the vision, drive the planning, and ride herd over the implementation of new processes, procedures, governance, and support systems. I believe this should be the responsibility of the senior marketing executive, as it offers that CMO an enormous opportunity to redefine and increase the relevance of his or her organization. If marketing management cannot step up to the plate, however, I have seen several sales operations departments grab the ball and become the lightning rod for a more limited transformation effort under the banner of "sales enablement."

- Clean up the existing mess quickly. In some ways, cleaning up the existing content is a lot like organizing the closets. First, look hard at what you have and throw away those things you really don't need. It's amazing how much content accumulates in marketing and sales repositories over time. But when people go through a systematic cleanup and rationalization process, much of that stuff is found to be inconsequential, outdated, and just flat wrong. Get rid of the content that is clearly unusable or outdated, and do it fast.

- Attack the low-hanging fruit. It will become clear during any cleanup and assessment that there are certain areas where a targeted solution to a specific problem will be embraced and quickly adopted by the sales organization. Some good examples of this are more systematic PowerPoint management processes, correspondence and proposal generation systems, and product configurators.

- Elicit help from outsiders. A company should not try to implement the VCCM without the support of some key vendors who need to get on board with the vision as partners.

  - If a company has committed to a specific sales training and methodology vendor, it is important for that vendor to adapt their methodology and consulting and training offerings to the marketing organization. If they have not done this, and look glassy-eyed when you attempt to discuss marketing and sales alignment and customer-centric, sales-ready content, get rid of them.

- Make sure that your CRM and Content Management vendors understand your objectives and strategy, and confirm that they have the technology infrastructure to support the Value-Mapping Process. Also discuss their long-term product plans to make sure they have a clear vision for improving marketing and sales effectiveness, as well as a technology road map that will support your vision.
- Make sure your marketing agency is on board. If they can be brought into the Value-Mapping Process, they will be far more productive and valuable to your enterprise over the long haul.

- Don't repeat the mistakes you made with CRM. Management must resist the temptation to look at the implementation of the VCCM primarily from a technology perspective. The VCCM is a strategic process and culture transformation effort, not just the implementation of a sales portal, a PowerPoint management system, or a proposal and collateral generation system. I contend that if technology is not viewed as a secondary consideration, costs will balloon, adoption will be slow and painful, and the chance for hitting a home run will be severely diminished. This is the hard lesson we all learned from our experiences with Customer Relationship Management, where the business vision and underlying process was often overshadowed by the belief that technology was the critical factor.

THINGS TO REMEMBER

There are several things to think about when implementing the Value-Centric Communications Model. Fortunately, it was designed with these things in mind:

- Your company is unique. As such, management needs to adopt the specific techniques, processes, tools, and best practices that best reflect your company's business model, channel structure, culture, and technology infrastructure.
- The twenty-first-century communication environment is continually evolving. As I mentioned in Part I, new Internet-enabled communications techniques, especially in the area of rich-media management and collaboration, are rapidly evolving. The good news is that the VCCM establishes a

framework for easily evaluating and adapting to new communications technologies and techniques.

- You can't manage all the content. No matter how well you implement the VCCM, some sales and marketing people will continue to create new content outside of the Integrated Knowledge and Content Repository. However, if you continuously improve both the Value Map and the Sanctioned Content, keeping it current, relevant, and valuable, salespeople will have little reason to morph that content or create their own presentations.

- Change takes time. Most companies can only tolerate change in small, digestible portions. Implementing the VCCM is often like replacing the parts in a race car during a race. You can't throw out everything and start from scratch, and you can't make all the changes at once or you will surely fall behind your competition. The component structure of the entire process model, however, enables companies to implement different best practices at their own pace in the context of a long-term strategic vision.

- Pareto's Principle applies—20 percent of the messages and content are used 80 percent of the time. The key is to determine which messages are really driving the business, and which content is really adding value to the sales process. Then, devote your resources to continuously improving and exploiting those specific message and content assets.

GUIDING PRINCIPLES

There are five guiding principles that managers should keep in mind as they implement the Value-Centric Communications Model:

1. Transfer knowledge; don't just disseminate information. The more you educate a person, the more you influence that person's thinking and behavior. To be effective, marketing and sales content needs to engage the reader and provide a productive learning experience. Marketing and sales professionals must understand that they are in the knowledge-transfer business, and that they are meant to do more than just disseminate information. They need to approach content development and delivery as a critical knowledge-transfer function with the end objective being how well the reader comprehends and retains the information, not how much information they delivered. This knowledge-transfer perspective has profound implications on the way messages and Sanctioned Content are created and delivered, and how marketing and sales organizations gather and share sales intelligence.

2. Less is more. Let's face the facts. Many people don't like to read anyway, and the resolution on computer screens, which can be many times worse

than paper, makes reading and absorbing information even more difficult. Following a Value Map will help ensure that marketing people invest their time in creating and managing content that is more relevant and valuable, which will help reduce a lot of the extraneous and superficial content that doesn't accelerate the marketing, selling, and buying process. The "less is more" philosophy that permeates the VCCM results in fewer documents, fewer PowerPoint slides, fewer Web pages, fewer words, fewer inconsistencies, and less duplication. In the end, this will significantly reduce the Total Cost of Content.

3. Embrace Web-Assisted Selling. It is critical for B-to-B companies to exploit all of the communication capabilities of the Internet and aggressively embrace Web-Assisted Selling as a fundamental component of their prospect and customer interaction strategy. Making this commitment will reduce costs, create closer proximity to their customers, and improve the quality and impact of all prospect and customer interactions. As I mentioned earlier, this new communication environment requires more collaboration between marketing and sales organizations and a much greater focus on coordinated communications programs. It also means that:

- Marketing must learn how to use the Web to have value-centric, two-way conversations with prospects during the demand-generation process so they can gather richer information before handing off prospects to salespeople.

- Sales organizations need to embrace Web conferencing as a primary prospect and customer communication mechanism, especially during the early stages of the sales cycle.

- Marketing needs to implement more collaborative selling tools, including guided selling systems, conjoint analysis, product configurators, and ROI calculators that help sales and sales support people really engage their customers and prospects.

- Companies need to create and manage critical portions of their content in smaller, more componentized chunks that can then be assembled on demand for more personalized, situation-specific content. The Value-Mapping Process will give many companies their first taste of this componentization process, and they should leverage this experience with other structured content, such as presentation and proposal generation systems. The long-term objective, however, is to enable the channels to use technology to dynamically assemble and generate a higher percentage of their day-to-day correspondence and to create more personalized, targeted, customer-facing collateral.

4. Increase the value of the channel. Sales channels are most effective when they are well informed about the marketplace, their customers' business problems, and how their customers use products and services to solve those problems. Those attributes help great salespeople have intelligent conversations with and deliver tangible value to their prospects and customers. As Glenn Shimkus of Amdocs said to me, "There is a direct linear relationship between sales success and the knowledge of the channel. In today's environment, the disintermediation of much of the face-to-face contact during the sales cycle has made every sales call more important than ever." And as Dennis Dunlap, CEO of the American Marketing Association, concludes, "The key is providing salespeople with the information that gives them every opportunity to have an intelligent conversation with a potential buyer."[1] As such, B-to-B companies need to ensure their salespeople really understand their customers' business issues, stay one step ahead of the market, ask the right questions at the right time, and add tangible value above and beyond the products and services in their customers' eyes. As Neil Racham, the founder of Spin Selling, says, "Sales forces that simply talk about the product are doomed to fail. Sales must begin to create customer value in order to survive."[2]

5. Assist your Internal Champions. Remember, a vast majority of the discussion, debate, and decision making about whether or not to buy a product happens when a salesperson is not in the room. To take advantage of this fact of life, marketing organizations should create collateral and tools that also make it easy for Internal Champions to carry the message forward in their organizations. This content should be fashioned in a way that educates the Internal Champion about the Complete Value Proposition while increasing his or her stature and credibility within the organization. Remember, the stronger and more influential your Internal Champion becomes, the more you will sell! There are also three important ancillary benefits that come from creating content for the Internal Champion:

- It results in more high-quality, customer- and value-centric collateral and selling tools.
- It secures the bond between the salesperson and the Internal Champion.
- It clarifies, hardens, and sharpens the Complete Value Propositions.

---

[1] Presentation at the American Marketing Association, Customer Message Management Forum, 12/12/02.

[2] *Selling Power Magazine* (Fredericksburg, Virginia: Summer, 2003).

CHAPTER 16

Building a Value Map

THE VALUE-MAPPING PROCESS HELPS marketing and sales organizations gain a deeper and more objective understanding of the specific business problems of their customers, the issues that concern the stakeholders they sell to, and a clear and factual understanding of the real value that their products and services deliver. As such, Value Maps are the raw materials that drive more sales-ready Sanctioned Content, and make the marketing and sales organizations a lot more focused on the customer.

Creating a single, clear, and concise view of all of the value a company provides its customers is the only way I know of to ensure that company's Sanctioned Content is truly customer-centric, and their marketing and salespeople are engaging the marketplace, their prospects, and their customers in a coordinated and cohesive fashion. This is why I believe Value Mapping has the potential to become a "killer app" for marketing and sales effectiveness, and why I predict it will be supported by most CRM and Content Management systems in the next few years.

THE ELEMENTS OF A VALUE MAP

A Value Map is nothing more than a small, centrally managed, and "internal eyes only" knowledge base of succinct facts, ideas, and insights, organized to clearly reflect the key elements of a company's Complete Value Propositions. In its most basic form, a Value Map is based upon a structured knowledge model that reflects the logical relationships between a company's solutions and the problems those solutions solve. The knowledge base is populated and continuously improved upon through a closed-loop workflow process that uses simple, fill-in-the-blank forms. These forms document the discrete elements of the different business objectives that prospects and customers have, as well as the specific pains and issues of the different stakeholders involved in the buying process. These discrete objective and pain elements are then linked to the specific capabilities of a company's solutions, with each link representing an opportunity for creating a Complete Value Proposition.

By systematically managing these critical knowledge assets in a single, central location, they can also serve as an intelligent front end or Smart Taxonomy for a company's Sanctioned Marketing and Sales Content, so all of the Core Intellectual Assets are more effectively leveraged to impact the entire marketing and sales process.

Value Maps are built around a two-level hierarchy (as shown in Figure 16.1) containing overriding strategic business objectives, such as "increasing marketing and sales effectiveness." These objectives can then be broken down into the multiple operational needs of different stakeholders, thereby reflecting the reality of the Cascading Need Phenomenon. This hierarchy facilitates more precise definitions of multiple customer business objectives and stakeholder pains, which are then mapped to the specific capabilities of a company's (and optionally a competitor's) solutions. This hierarchy provides a framework enabling companies to capture more specific information on how those different pains are addressed by the different capabilities of their solutions. Complete Value Proposition forms are automatically generated at each intersection between a pain and a capability, and these forms help subject matter experts come up with Best Answers to specific questions about how the actual value is created, described, differentiated, and ultimately validated.

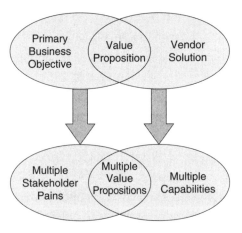

FIGURE 16.1 *THE VALUE MAP HIERARCHY*

THE VALUE MAPPING FORMS

The Value Mapping knowledge base is created by filling out a couple of simple FAQ template forms for each stakeholder pain. These forms are generic in nature so they can be applied to any solutions-centric selling methodology. These templates can contain four different things depending on how complete a company wants its Value Maps to be:

1. Checklists segmenting solutions, capabilities, business objectives, and stakeholder pains so they can be sorted and selected by a variety of characteristics

2. Logical links between pains and capabilities

3. Best Answers to the critical questions that both marketing and salespeople need to understand in order to be fluent on the customer objectives and stakeholder pains and how customers actually use the company's solutions to solve those problems and pains

4. Best practices for salespeople, including best questions to ask and best actions to take to accelerate the selling and buying process

THE BASIC VALUE MAP

Even the most basic Value Map can provide considerable benefits because it clearly and succinctly documents the essence of a company's business in one place. It gives everybody in the enterprise—from the CEO to the salespeople—the same answers to the following questions:

- What business objectives do our products and services address?
- Who are the stakeholders who are most affected by those objectives?
- What are the specific pains these stakeholders face?
- Which of our solutions and capabilities meet those business objectives and pains?

There are five elements of a Basic Value Map (see Figure 16.2) that enable it to be built in a just couple of hours:

1. Short descriptions and checklists that identify and segment the customer's business objectives and the specific needs of the individual stakeholders

2. Short descriptions and checklists that identify the solutions and capabilities that address those business objectives and pains

FIGURE 16.2 THE BASIC VALUE MAP

3. Short descriptions of the value that is created at the intersections between pains and capabilities

4. Links to appropriate Sanctioned Content so that people can instanta-neously jump from the short descriptions to more detailed information

5. A closed-loop workflow process that ensures continuous improvement of the knowledge in the Value Map

THE COMPLETE VALUE MAP

Once a company has implemented a Basic Value Map, it can easily be improved upon by adding the concept of Best Answers to the Value Map-ping forms so subject matter experts can precisely document how value is created and quantified, how value is validated and proven, and how the solution is differentiated from the competition and other alternatives avail-able to prospects and customers.

The FAQ format of the Value Mapping forms and the workflow process make it very easy for product managers and subject matter experts to fill in the blanks over time and constantly improve upon the Best Answers. This makes the Value Map more complete and increasingly valuable to marketing

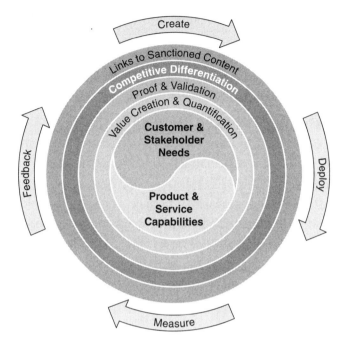

FIGURE 16.3 *THE COMPLETE VALUE MAP*

and sales professionals. The questions that make up a Complete Value Map (see Figure 16.3) include:

- What are the causes of these different business objectives and stakeholder pains and needs?
- What are the risks and implications of not acting on them now?
- What are the alternatives available to address them?
- How does a stakeholder use a specific capability of our solution to address their specific pains and needs and create value?
- What are the specific and quantifiable benefits that the customer and stakeholder will gain from that specific capability?
- How do we prove that our capabilities address the specific needs and substantiate the actual amount of value that is created?
- How do we factually document our competitive differentiation in a way that ties that differentiation directly to value?

The links to the Sanctioned Content on a Complete Value Map reinforce the Best Answers so salespeople can quickly jump to relevant white papers, presentations, references, success stories, industry analyst reports, or even ROI calculators, all managed outside of the Value Map.

INTEGRATED SALES COACHING

Finally, Complete Value Maps can easily be enhanced with sales intelligence and best sales practices to create a valuable sales coaching system (see Figure 16.4) that delivers just-in-time advice, selling tips, and silver bullets to salespeople in the context of a particular sales situation or stakeholder issue. Many studies on sales effectiveness confirm that the best salespeople have extensive situational knowledge and intuitively know the right things to say and the right things to do given different selling situations. For the first time, Value Maps provide companies with a tool that can help sales

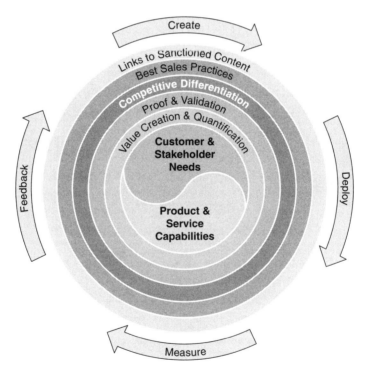

FIGURE 16.4 INTEGRATED SALES COACHING

organizations catalogue this situational knowledge, thereby coaching the average salesperson into behaving like a top performer on a regular basis.

For example, a well-constructed Complete Value Map enhanced with best selling practices and other sales intelligence can dynamically generate a pre-call cheat sheet for a salesperson. It outlines specific questions to ask and tactics to try based upon:

- The specific stakeholder he or she is calling on
- The particular industry that person is in
- The different business issues that person should be interested in
- The specific competitors involved

This cheat sheet can arm the salesperson with rich situational knowledge, suggested tactics, and silver bullets that will enable them to have a much more intelligent and insightful conversation with their prospect or customer regarding their specific business issues and the value provided by the solution and the company.

BEST VALUE MAPPING PRACTICES

There are several best practices that should be adopted to improve the quality, thoroughness, and impact of the Value-Mapping Process:

- Start with collaboration. This is best accomplished through a meeting of the most experienced marketing and sales professionals to develop the initial version of the Value Map. These meetings are often intense, as people grapple with the hard issues surrounding actual value and differentiation, but the pain is worth the effort.

- Focus on the customer objectives, needs, and pains first. The best Value-Mapping efforts start out by identifying the key facts, insights, and ideas that comprise the specific stakeholder pains and needs that a company's solutions solve. Once this knowledge has been agreed upon, segmented, and codified, the mapping process should shift its focus to solutions and capabilities, then differentiation, and finally proof. Incorporating best sales practices and coaching should only be implemented after the Value Map has been in use for some period and shaken down.

- Demand clarity. Clarity breeds controversy, and as I just mentioned, the best Value-Mapping sessions are often intense and emotional, as marketing and sales professionals grapple with the precise value their companies actually provide and how they are truly different from their competitors. It is important to force precision and clarity of the Best Answers in these Value-Mapping sessions, and often it's a good practice to have a neutral facilitator to drive the process and ensure that difficult issues are brought up and hard questions are answered. The ultimate objective of the process is to harden the value propositions so they stand up to the scrutiny of the most critical skeptic in the meeting.

- Use a relational model. Value Maps are made up of structured chunks of content. As such, basic Value Maps can be built manually with MS Word™ templates and standard Web technology, using HTML and hyper-links to connect the various forms in the Value Map in a logical fashion. I have also seen companies create basic Value Maps using a structured PowerPoint database, which can then be enhanced with audio sales coaching. Complete Value Maps, however, have to be built using a content management technology that supports a more relational data model. The discrete elements of the map must be managed in a way that more naturally reflects how those elements logically relate to the other elements of the map. The advantages of using a relational data model for the Value Map are significant:

  - The model can more easily be expanded and enhanced over time as needs dictate.
  - Because they are only stored once, the individual elements, Best Answers, and best practices can be easily updated and changed with simple input forms as the business and competitive landscapes evolve and new knowledge is uncovered.
  - It enables the implementation of a closed-loop feedback and knowledge-sharing capability at the element level, so the knowledge base is continually improved upon.
  - It enables multiple reports and views of the information, including situational pre-call cheat sheets and follow-up correspondence for salespeople. It can also generate the graphical Value Maps I described in Part II for marketing professionals and product managers, enabling them to better manage all of their intellectual property assets.
  - Individual elements, Best Answers, and best practices can easily be linked to more detailed Sanctioned Content that supports the specific elements, including product descriptions, reference stories, white papers, PowerPoint presentations, competitive analysis, or even selling tools like ROI calculators.

The good news is that the data model for a complete Value Map is not rocket science. It can be implemented with most modern Enterprise Content Management systems and tightly integrated into a company's Customer Relationship Management system. Unfortunately, as I write this book, most ECM and CRM vendors do not provide native support for Value Mapping in their products. But I believe that rudimentary Value Maps with some basic sales coaching capability will soon become an integral part of every CRM system so that the Value Map can be accessed through the same screens that salespeople use every day. This will happen as companies start demanding a coherent marketing and sales effectiveness vision, as well as the technology strategy to support that vision, from their CRM vendors.

- Classify the value propositions. One of the most effective Value-Mapping techniques is classifying the value that companies provide into different categories. After a lot of trial and error, I have concluded that almost all value propositions for B-to-B products can be classified into one of two different categories:
  - The reduction of cost, time, effort, and risk
  - The increase in revenue, production, quality, or competitive advantage

    Some people will argue that these two categories are not mutually exclusive. For example, increasing revenues with the same resources reduces the cost of revenue generation. Over the years, however, I have found that most people don't make that distinction. When they feel a pain, they usually see and verbalize it in terms of one of these two factors.

- View your business model as a product. Since it is getting harder and harder to create visible product differentiation, it is important for companies to look at the way they do business as a value add. By putting your business practices into the Value Map, you can create value propositions around the way you do business that can often make more of a difference to customers than a differentiated product. This practice also forces management to look at different ways to improve the overall value proposition and establish practices that visibly enhance the company's competitive advantage.

- Force ownership and accountability. The entire Value-Mapping Process should be owned by a "C" level executive, preferably the vice-president of marketing, as part of an overall customer-centricity strategy. This executive should have a team of subject matter experts, each responsible for specific portions of the Value Map. Usually the best people to do this are the product marketing managers, as they should be the most knowledgeable people in the enterprise about the specific customer needs that their individual products solve. When product managers embrace the Value-Mapping Process, a wonderful thing happens: They start competing with each other for the mind share of the channels by improving the value of their products and creating better value propositions, instead of relying on superficial internal merchandizing tactics that many of them use today to promote their products.

- Review the map regularly. Value Mapping is an iterative process, and a key component of this process should be periodic reviews by the owner to ensure the map is kept up-to-date and accurate. Since the Value Map is just a set of checklists, questions, and answers, it usually takes about an hour or so a month to keep it current, even for the most complex solutions. I recommend formalizing these periodic reviews, requiring a sign-off procedure. Most modern content management systems can facilitate this process with content expiration dates in the meta-data.

- Make the Value Map your primary marketing and sales taxonomy. Companies should use the Value Map as the primary topology to organize all other marketing and sales content. By organizing all marketing and sales content according to the customer's business objectives, stakeholder issues, and the value that your products and services provide, you are constantly reinforcing the customer's point of view and creating a more customer-centric culture. Linking the elements of the Value Map to the content in the Integrated Knowledge and Content Repository will also reduce the amount of duplication and morphing that goes on because the morphed and duplicated content will not have links, making it tougher to find.

- Encourage feedback. One of the most important aspects of a Value Map is a simple, integrated feedback process that enables marketing and sales professionals to continuously improve the value proposition as well as the sales intelligence. This feedback loop should be monitored, and people who provide insights and share their knowledge should be recognized and somehow rewarded by management.

- Add a glossary. Another simple but valuable feature that can be added to a Value Map is an interactive, context-sensitive glossary of the key terms used. This contextual knowledge can significantly assist the salesperson in having a more intelligent and insightful conversation with prospects and customers.

For more information on Value Mapping, and samples of the templates and forms to construct a Value Map, please see my Web site, http://www. web2one.com.

CHAPTER 17

Optimizing the Sanctioned Content

A S I MENTIONED IN THE PREVIOUS CHAPTER, the Value-Mapping Process is built around a closed-loop workflow for developing and continually improving the raw material knowledge assets of a marketing and sales organization. The other workflow process of the Value-Centric Communications Model is the Content Optimization Framework. This is a closed-loop process that helps management identify and organize the best practices for more effectively managing the finished goods Sanctioned Content.

As Figure 17.1 shows, the framework systematically addresses four key, inter-related aspects that blend together and often overlap with each other. For example, rationalizing the content often improves the quality of the content as well as the user's delivery experience.

The ultimate objective of these processes is to make the Sanctioned Content more valuable to customers and salespeople. This will eliminate a lot of the duplication, morphing, and rogue content development that drives the Total Cost of Content through the roof.

It's been my observation that salespeople usually complain about two things when it comes to the content developed by marketing:

1. It doesn't focus on the right issues, which is the most common complaint.
2. It focuses on the right issue, but it is not effective.

The Value-Mapping Process helps solve the first problem by getting everybody on the same page about what needs to be conveyed. The Content Optimization Framework ensures that the Value Map is reflected in the Sanctioned Content, and that the content is constantly being improved upon so that it is as effective as it can be.

For example, let's say your company has decided it needs to improve the way you create, manage, and deliver presentations. By looking at the various PowerPoint management and delivery options available to you in light of

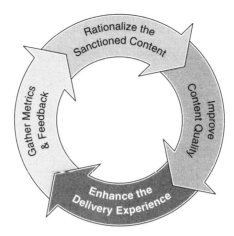

FIGURE 17.1 CONTENT OPTIMIZATION FRAMEWORK

the four aspects of the Content Optimization Model, you can answer the following key questions:

- What presentation content do we really need?
- How can we best integrate our presentation materials with our other marketing and sales content?
- What can we do to continuously improve the quality and impact of our PowerPoint assets?
- How should we organize our presentation content?
- How can we exploit our presentation assets to help our sales channels deliver more tangible value to prospects and customers?
- How can we better leverage our presentation assets through different synchronous and asynchronous delivery options, including e-mail, Windows Media, Flash, and Web conferencing?
- How do we measure the benefits we get from this initiative?

The rest of this chapter describes some of the best ideas and practices for each aspect of the model that I uncovered during my research for *Escaping the Black Hole*. Hopefully, a few of them will resonate with you and provide you with some ideas you can use to get the ball rolling in your own company.

RATIONALIZING THE SANCTIONED CONTENT

Once a company has created a Value Map, they need to begin to restructure and better organize their Sanctioned Content.

FIGURE 17.2 CONTENT RATIONALIZATION

The objectives of this rationalization process (shown in Figure 17.2) are:

- To create a more balanced architecture for the Sanctioned Content, and to define a plan to implement that architecture
- To ensure that the Sanctioned Content reflects the knowledge in the Value Map
- To reduce the Total Cost of the Sanctioned Content by:
  - Getting rid of outdated, erroneous, and redundant content
  - Reducing the overall amount of Sanctioned Content
  - Better organizing the Sanctioned Content to simplify life for the salespeople and partner channels, thereby making them more effective
- To identify processes for managing that Sanctioned Content as the new initiatives move forward

While every company will approach this rationalization process differently, there are three different techniques for formulating a sensible strategy:

1. Eliminating the multiple content silos
2. Rationalizing the physical composition of the content
3. Rationalizing the logical composition of the content

By adopting these three perspectives, management will be able to create a clearer plan to reduce their Total Cost of Content and improve the impact of their Sanctioned Content on the revenue-generation process.

ELIMINATING CONTENT SILOS One of the most important benefits of creating a 360-degree view of Sanctioned Content is that it helps reduce the significant waste and inefficiencies that come with out-of-date, erroneous, and redundant information stored in multiple places. Some larger companies I interviewed had more than a hundred different sites and newsletters containing marketing and sales content. Several of these companies had initiated projects to review and assess the value of these different sites, and found that most of the sites contained a lot of duplicate, erroneous, out-dated, and even contradictory information.

For better or worse, anybody with a budget can create a Web site or product newsletter, and this often fuels what I call the "dueling product manager syndrome." Product managers often have to fight with each other for the mind share of the sales channels. The result can be an explosion in the number of internal Web sites and newsletters that can confuse the sales channels and dramatically increase the Total Cost of Content.

Systematically managing all Sanctioned Content around a Value Map, on the other hand, helps companies contain and control this explosion of content silos through a combination of the 360-degree view and processes that govern the creation of Web sites and content. The ideal result, as Figure 17.3 indicates, is a substantial reduction in the total amount of content by eliminating redundancy and duplication.

Here are a couple of best practices I have seen companies implement in the last several years as they tried to eliminate redundant and un-useful content:

- The first is to layer the Sanctioned Content and adopt a hierarchical view that encompasses both the internal-facing and external-facing content. As

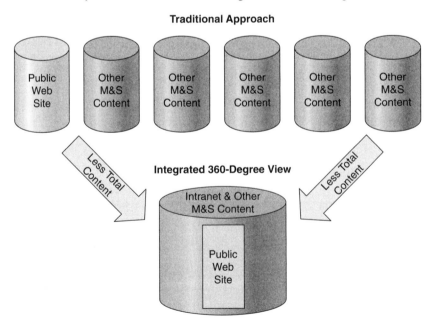

FIGURE 17.3 ELIMINATING REDUNDANT AND UN-USEFUL CONTENT

shown in Figure 17.3, the company's Intranet is both a logical and physical extension of their public Web site. In this hierarchical view, the company's public Web site becomes the central Sanctioned Content asset for customer-facing content. The internal Sanctioned Content, including the Value Map, is logically and physically managed in a secure fashion on the company's Intranet so that it reinforces, not duplicates, the customer-facing content on the public Web site.

- The second best practice is to implement portal functionality to create a single access point for all of the knowledge and content assets. EDS, for example, created a portal hierarchy for both their customers and employees that was highly successful in eliminating duplicate and inconsistent information and creating a more cohesive and productive communications and knowledge-transfer environment for both groups.

- The third best practice is to establish a short-term archiving process for the Sanctioned Content you are eliminating. If nobody complains after six months, this content can be permanently discarded.

RATIONALIZING THE PHYSICAL COMPOSITION When establishing a long-term architecture for Sanctioned Content, companies should segment that content by its physical composition so they can then begin to change the overall makeup over time and:

- Increase the percentage of rich media, including PowerPoint, Flash, and Windows Media, for external as well as internal Sanctioned Content
- Systematically increase the amount of componentized, configurable, and customizable content so more of it can be easily assembled and dynamically generated both by the marketing team and the sales channels

By taking this physical view of their Sanctioned Content, management can more easily determine an ideal structural composition for their particular culture, business model, and technology infrastructure. Once the vision for the ideal physical makeup of their Sanctioned Content is established, they can then set milestones and benchmarks for achieving that ideal over time.

Increasing the percentage of rich-media content. Today, a lot of forward-looking B-to-B companies are incorporating rich-media presentations into their public Web sites to improve the user's learning experience and ensure that their messages are more effectively delivered and reinforced through the combination of visual and audio content. Eventually, most B-to-B marketing and sales organizations will replace a lot of their text-based documents with richer audio-visual media, and they will enhance their critical presentation material with audio narrations to more effectively and more consistently deliver the value proposition messages. It is interesting to note that the companies I talked to who had narrated their key messages in PowerPoint slides experienced less morphing of their presentations by the sales channels.

This increase in the use of rich media will happen naturally as customers demand a more compelling knowledge-transfer experience, and as PowerPoint continues to evolve as a dominant communication medium for complex business concepts and information. However, these rich-media assets will need to be more aggressively managed to reduce redundancy and control message morphing, and that requires an enterprise strategy for managing and controlling presentation material and other rich-media assets. It also means that these assets need to be more tightly integrated with delivery technologies, like Web conferencing, so that salespeople can make better Web-assisted selling calls.

Another thing I discovered during my research was an increasing use of Flash (as opposed to Windows Media) for creating and delivering rich-media presentations. While I am not a technologist, the people I spoke to gave me several reasons for this trend. They felt that:

- Flash had better support for non-Windows operating systems.
- Flash had better internal performance.
- Flash provided a richer visual environment.
- Flash supported more interactivity with the user, which enabled people to create a more personalized and compelling knowledge-transfer experience.

Fortunately, the technology to add narrations to PowerPoint slides and to automatically generate Flash as well as Windows Media presentations from those slides is now available from companies like Avitage! (http://www.avitage.com/) and others. When you add this enhanced rich-media creation functionality to the ability to manage individual PowerPoint slides and other rich-media assets at an enterprise level, the potential implications are significant. The pieces have finally come together for marketing and sales organizations to not only exploit their rich-media assets, but also to minimize the duplication and inconsistencies that come from the morphing of those assets.

Increasing the amount of componentized content. The second aspect that companies need to focus on as they rationalize the physical composition of their Sanctioned Content is to systematically increase the percentage of componentized content over time. Componentization requires content to be more structured and repeatable. As we will see later, this not only facilitates the customization of the content deliverable, but it also improves the quality. Personalization was the first stage of this customization process and there is little doubt that the future of marketing and sales content lies in smaller components that can be maintained in one place, and then be assembled, either automatically or manually, to fit a specific person and situation. As Aberdeen research reported in 2002, the best companies are adopting "a 'change once/update everywhere' paradigm, wherein changes to product, customer, or market information are instantaneously promulgated throughout the marketing/sales enterprise."[1]

The fact is that B-to-B companies will be required to componentize an increasing amount of their content in the future in order to remain competitive and to provide the support their sales channels will come to expect. Componentizing marketing and sales content will also increase the alignment between marketing and sales professionals, as it will give each of these groups more control of the deliverable and less to argue about. If the Sanctioned Content is componentized and organized correctly, salespeople will have greater flexibility and feel like they are more in control of what gets delivered to the customer. Conversely, marketing professionals will be able to ensure that:

- Salespeople are not creating their own content.
- Customer-facing presentations are not being morphed beyond recognition.
- Branding activities are being consistently reinforced.

---

[1]"Bridging the Great Divide: Process, Technology, and the Marketing/Sales Interface," research published by Aberdeen Group (Wellesley, Massachusetts: 2002).

Unfortunately, componentization requires a lot of discipline on everybody's part, as well as a whole new way of writing so that components come together without sounding contrived and artificial. Because of this, I have come to believe that componentization is a long-term process, evolving through a series of small, logical steps that begin to teach people the benefits of componentization. Four of the easiest ways to start this process and begin experimenting with componentized content are to:

1. Create your Value Map using a database so that the individual elements of the Complete Value Propositions and best sales practices are managed as components. Because the Value Map is based upon a pre-established checklist and FAQ template, this will enable you to immediately create situation-specific sales coaching forms and also customizable follow-up correspondence. For example, a data-driven Value Map can be used to automatically generate issue-specific follow-up e-mails to ensure that the business issues, value propositions, and next steps discussed in the sales call are documented in a professional and consistent fashion. By integrating the Value Map with the CRM system, this correspondence can also be recorded and incorporated into the opportunity and pipeline management system to show what actually has been sent to the prospect or customer.

2. Implement an enterprise presentation management system that manages sanctioned presentation content at the individual slide level, and provides an easy process for salespeople to assemble customized presentations. A key quality of such a system is that it should be seamlessly integrated with multiple delivery platforms, such as Web conferencing and the automatic generation of Windows Media and Flash vignettes.

3. Implement a simple proposal generation system. According to Robert F. Kantin in his book *Strategic Proposals,* "In many cases, as much as 80 percent of a proposal is standard wording."[2] When managed in a componentized fashion, this standard 80 percent can be used and re-used in a variety of content, including Web sites, proposals, letters, presentations, and e-mails, ensuring accuracy and consistency.

4. Finally, just-in-time learning systems offer a lot of potential for componentizing content so that important enterprise knowledge is leveraged as much as it can be. Cisco, for example, has implemented an enterprise-wide

---

[2]Robert F. Kantin, *Strategic Proposals: Closing the Big Deal* (Vantage Press, 1999).

knowledge-transfer initiative that involves maximizing the use of what it calls Reusable Learning Objects or RLOs. These can be dynamically configured to support the particular needs of each employee on a just-in-time basis.

RATIONALIZING THE LOGICAL COMPOSITION After companies have developed a plan for reducing the number of content silos and rationalizing the physical makeup of their Sanctioned Content over time, they should also implement a process for assessing and organizing that content logically. Sanctioned Content should be segmented by its purpose and orientation, not only its physical characteristics. By combining this logical perspective with the physical perspective, management can create a more intelligent long-term architecture for the Sanctioned Content. As Figure 17.4 indicates, this will help reduce the total amount of content, while at the same time ensuring that:

• The Sanctioned Content reflects the Value Map by being more customer-centric and aligned with the marketing and selling process.

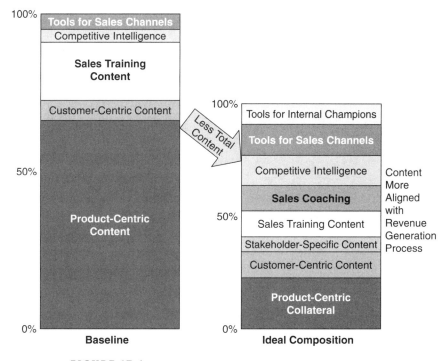

FIGURE 17.4 RATIONALIZING THE LOGICAL COMPOSITION

- There are more Web-based selling tools to serve the needs of all sales channels as well as Internal Champions.
- Sales training and competitive intelligence content is continually improved upon.

There are several techniques and best practices that will help companies more logically rationalize their Sanctioned Content and achieve these three objectives:

Increasing stakeholder and sales process alignment. One of the fundamental tenets of the Value-Centric Communications Model is that an increasing percentage of content and collateral should be focused on, and written from, the perspective of different stakeholders and customer constituencies. By using the Value Map to determine what content needs to be created, more stakeholder-specific and value-centric content will naturally evolve, and it will eliminate the development of any content that is extraneous to the communication of Complete Value Propositions.

As Figure 17.5 indicates, the Sanctioned Content targeted for specific stakeholders in the customer organization can also be segmented by the specific stages of the revenue-generation process. It is this intersection between the content assets and the process that ties the Buyer-Centric Revenue Acceleration Model to the Value-Centric Content and Communication Model,

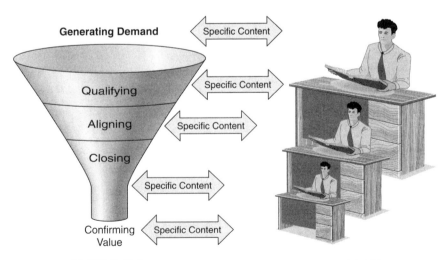

FIGURE 17.5 TARGET MULTIPLE STAKEHOLDERS AND STAGES

making the Synchronized Marketing and Sales Ecosystem a reality. As Joe Galvin of the Gartner Group told me: "Marketing needs to provide meaningful content that is tied to specific people at the different stages of the selling process. Salespeople need flexible and dynamic content to meet the challenges of different selling situations. This allows companies to really make their salespeople powerful."

Examples of stage-specific content would include presentation slides, qualifying questions, needs development tools, and closing tools like ROI systems. As Scott Santucci of BluePrint Marketing (http://www.blueprintmarketing.com/) told me, "A program to make decision makers aware of their problems is dramatically different than helping them figure out how to solve their problems." The good news is that with today's content management technologies, it is easy to tag this content so that it is aligned with specific stages of the selling process.

Figure 17.5 also shows another important integration touch point at the Value Confirmation stage where marketing programs and content can be created to help salespeople deal with the phenomenon of buyer's remorse. This Value Confirmation stage has become more important than ever because in many B-to-B companies, an increasing amount of business is coming from existing accounts. As such, marketing professionals and salespeople must invest more time on post-sales activities and consistently confirm that their existing customers appreciate all the value they are getting for their money. Cisco, for example, has implemented a mandatory quarterly value confirmation and review process for key accounts that has paid big results in renewals and has helped the company maintain its margins. This process was driven by the marketing organization, which created a complete program with special value confirmation content and sales support tools. Their approach allowed the sales channel to effectively execute this process through a structured, high-quality sales call with the customer. The result? Happier customers, happier salespeople, higher margins, and lots of new sales leads and opportunities.

Increasing the amount of selling tools and designing them so they can be used by Internal Champions. As I mentioned in a previous chapter, one of the core principles of the Value-Centric Communications Model is to increase the value of the salespeople. The best way to achieve this is to equip the channels with Web-Assisted Selling tools that help them:

- Use Web conferencing to have more intelligent and substantive interactions with customers during the needs development process
- Do a better job at sales call follow-up with professional-looking and value-based e-mails that can be directly generated from the Value Map and integrated with the Opportunity Management module of the CRM system
- Generate more compelling cost justifications and ROI scenarios
- Create more professional-looking proposals

Not only will these selling tools make salespeople more effective and help them deliver value to the customer, but they will also make those salespeople more efficient. For example, a recent Gartner Group study reported that "Enterprises that adopt a proposal generation system will cut in half the time it takes to create, edit, approve, and produce a professional-looking proposal."[3]

During my research for this book, I heard about some impressive success stories from companies who were beginning to implement systems where their sales and sales support people used the Web in their selling interactions with prospects customers. While these companies did not want to be identified by name for competitive advantage reasons, some of the results were indeed impressive:

- A large technology vendor that was implementing an enterprise presentation management system integrated with a Web conferencing engine calculated they would save more than $50 million in travel costs alone through effective use of Web presentations, while freeing up more than 75,000 sales and sales support days in the process.
- A major communications company that had designed a Web-based guided selling system produced the following results during the pilot project:
  - 100 to 700 percent increase in the number of proposals generated
  - 100 to 200 percent increase in the average value per proposal
  - 100 to 300 percent increase in the number of bookings
  - 200 to 400 percent increase in the average booking value

---

[3]Research published by the Gartner Group.

- A Fortune 100 financial services company saved more than 50 percent of the time it took salespeople to create presentations and follow-up correspondence.
- A global delivery company cut their average proposal generation time from three hours to forty-five minutes and increased close rates by more than 10 percent.
- A major enterprise services firm increased their average deal size and new customer close rate by more than 20 percent.

Finally, the sales and sales support people who were participating in these implementations are raving about their experience:

- 100 percent said that Web-Assisted Selling would reduce their need for sales support.
- 75 percent said they could close more deals every month.
- 91 percent said Web-Assisted Selling made them more effective.[4]

In the future, salespeople will demand more Web-based tools, and the companies that begin to experiment with these next-generation tools now will have the advantage in recruiting and retaining the best sales talent in the coming years.

But creating great Web-Assisted Selling tools for salespeople is not enough in this new competitive environment where a lot of the selling is also done by Internal Champions. As a result, sales tools should be designed to be intuitive. A person with little or no training should be able to perform the basic functions, allowing Internal Champions to leverage them in their private discussions with other stakeholders. Some of the best tools I have seen for Internal Champions include:

- Answers to the major objections they will get when the salesperson is not present
- A list of killer questions to ask and traps to lay for the competition
- Tools that help them structure and control the internal decision process
- Checklists that help them influence other stakeholders

---

[4]Statistics compiled by the American Marketing Association, http://www.marketingpower.com, December, 2004.

- Specific selling tools, such as ROI calculators or PowerPoint presentations, that have what I call a telescoping architecture. This is where a subset of the same tool that the salesperson uses can be given to the Internal Champions so they can leverage some of the basic functions of the tool in their internal selling efforts with minimal or no training.

Restructuring the sales intelligence. One of the most important aspects of the content rationalization process, however, is the long-term restructuring of the way sales training is done and internal sales intelligence is shared and leveraged. With the advances in distance learning techniques, plus the logistical costs and loss of selling days, most companies are limiting or even eliminating traditional training events. What haven't been eliminated in many of these companies, however, are the complex selling manuals or sales guides that traditionally accompanied these in-person sales training events.

While these sales guides are now stored online instead of on salespeople's shelves, my research indicates that many of them have become even larger and more cumbersome as product marketing managers try to make up for the lack of face-to-face training. There are several problems with this approach. First of all, these large, complex selling guides are very expensive to create and, like all large documents, virtually impossible to maintain and keep current. The end result is that most of these complex sales guides get a quick review by the channel, and then become "virtual shelf ware" instead of collecting real dust like they used to.

The Value-Centric Communications Model establishes a whole new vision for the sales training function. Instead of being event driven, and creating large training guides and manuals, sales trainers should become the champions and facilitators for a robust knowledge sharing and continuous learning environment built around a Value Map. In this environment, best practices, insights, and other sales intelligence will be managed in smaller, more componentized chunks. The information will be electronically delivered to salespeople in the context of the specific activity and sales situation they are engaged in at that particular time.

In stepping up to this challenge, the training department will become an agent of culture change, and they will need to figure out and implement reward and recognition systems to encourage knowledge sharing throughout the marketing and sales organization. One of the best ways to get started is for the sales training function to begin to sponsor internal discussion groups and blogs devoted to a particular subject, perhaps specific competitors, the sales process, or the compensation plan.

Another way to dramatically reduce the amount of formalized sales training guides is to add more sales intelligence, best practices, and sales coaching to the Value Map. Remember, the Value-Mapping Process has an integrated feedback loop for salespeople to submit insights and best practices, so this shared sales intelligence gets better and better over time. This focus on knowledge sharing and continuous improvement is a critical part of the process.

Finally, the sales training function should facilitate an environment where subject matter experts regularly add their insights to customer-facing content in a secure fashion, so that only salespeople can access these insights. This integration of internal and external information reduces the total amount of content required, and it eliminates a lot of redundancy and inconsistencies. It also dramatically improves selling effectiveness with just-in-time delivery of sales tips and best practices in the context of a specific sales situation and the customer business problem. Examples of adding coaching and sales intelligence to customer-facing content include:

- Adding secure coaching audio to PowerPoint slides. With this, the subject matter expert coaches the salesperson on how best to deliver that specific slide. As companies use more and more visuals to deliver their messages, this audio coaching will become one of the most effective training techniques available. Once the insights of the experts have been captured electronically, the potential uses of this asset are significant. Imagine the following scenario: As a salesperson prepares for a critical presentation, he or she assembles the slides for the presentation, and then downloads the audio coaching to an MP3 player to get coaching while driving to the customer's site.

- Adding audio or text coaching to a customer-facing Web page. With today's content management technologies, it is also easy to create a button on an "internal eyes only" version of a Web page, which can then launch either a textual or audio coaching object. In fact, the same audio coaching that was attached to a PowerPoint slide could also be attached to a graphical Web page or white paper so that this expert knowledge is fully leveraged over multiple pieces of Sanctioned Content.

- Finally, all of the Web-based selling tools should have a good, context-sensitive help system to ensure that both the salesperson and Internal Champions get the most out of the tool.

IMPROVING CONTENT QUALITY

As I mentioned in Part I, B-to-B marketing and sales organizations are in the knowledge-transfer business. As such, the topic of content quality should be answered from the perspective of:

- How quickly customers, prospects, and salespeople assimilate and comprehend the content
- How long they retain the key information
- How much the content changes their beliefs and behavior

The Content Optimization Framework includes a component for implementing quality-centric processes that help companies continuously improve the quality and effectiveness of the Sanctioned Content from these three perspectives (see Figure 17.6).

When you look at the quality of marketing and sales content from a knowledge-transfer perspective, there are four dimensions that should be considered during the content development process. I call these dimensions "the Four Ps" of content quality. As companies implement the VCCM, they should make sure content developers keep these four principles front and center:

1. Pertinence: The more relevant and pertinent the content is to readers, the more they will absorb and retain the information. There are two factors that always increase the pertinence of content:
   - The apparent timeliness of the information. The fresher the information seems, the more attention it gets. This means that content should regularly be refreshed so that it appears timely.

FIGURE 17.6 IMPROVING CONTENT QUALITY

- The uniqueness of the content. Content that offers new information and provocative ideas and insights is always more seductive and valuable than content that says the exact same thing others are saying. This is why it is important for companies to clearly document their differentiation in their Value Map, and merchandise that differentiation as much as possible.

2. Precision: The clearer and more specific the information, the easier it is to understand and remember. One way to ensure precision and clarity is to think about content from the perspective of Internal Champions. They need precise content to understand and carry the key messages forward.

3. Personalization: The more that content is personalized, the more receptive the reader is to the ideas and information presented.

4. Production: We are all becoming more sophisticated content consumers, and as such, the professionalism and production value of the content often impacts how much credibility we give it. This has always been true with textual material where poor organization and misspelling can affect the reader's perceptions. Today, however, as more and more rich-media content is being created, the production quality has become an important issue. It is very easy to look amateurish if you don't produce professional quality rich-media content.

Additionally, customers and prospects are getting smarter and smarter every day, now that they have 24-7 access to all kinds of information. I contend that this puts a premium on candor. Sanctioned Content must be honest and forthright, acknowledge any weaknesses, and try not to over-hype strengths.

It often goes against human nature to admit a weakness, but I have found that one of the most effective ways to gain credibility with prospects and customers is to admit to a minor weakness in a product or service, and then mitigate it. The reason candor is so effective is that it disarms the reader, creating a foundation of trust, credibility, and believability. This is why it is important to clearly identify weaknesses as well as strengths during the Value-Mapping Process, so that you can implement a strategy to either improve a specific weakness or minimize it.

In the last few years I have observed several well-established content development techniques and best practices that will improve the quality of the Sanctioned Content as well as the knowledge-transfer experience. As content development and communication technologies evolve over the next several years, I am confident that more good ideas will emerge.

IMPROVING THE QUALITY OF TEXT

There are three overriding content development strategies that management can emphasize and reinforce to dramatically improve the quality of the text-based content:

1. Structure the content in a consistent fashion.
2. Use stories whenever possible.
3. Write the content in small, easily digestible chunks, such as bullets and FAQs.

STRUCTURING THE CONTENT Applying a consistent and repeatable structure to textual information is more important than ever because of the volume of text that's being created, and the fact that a lot of this text is being delivered through computer screens, which are much harder to read than paper. Increasing the structure of textual content through the use of templates and more formalized content development and writing techniques provides several important benefits:

- A consistent content structure simplifies the creation and ongoing maintenance of that content. This will also lay the groundwork should you want to dynamically generate that content in the future.
- Structure enhances creativity. It breeds new insights and ideas, and establishes a framework that facilitates the sharing of knowledge.
- A consistent structure gives the reader a contextual perspective that often increases comprehension and retention of the information.
- Structure forces readers down a path that makes it easier for them to "buy into" the message, which enhances the content's ability to influence their thinking and behavior.

Today's content development technologies, including Microsoft Word and PowerPoint, make it easy for companies to create standard templates for much of their content. There are also proven content development methodologies, such as Information Mapping (www.infomap.com), that can be adopted at an enterprise level to help a company's content developers improve the quality of the written word.

Information Mapping is a systematic content organization, structuring, and writing methodology that was first developed in the 1970s. This methodology has been implemented in many large enterprises over the years, and there have been several studies on the effects of this more systematic approach to structured content both for paper documents as well as electronic content delivered through Web sites. And as you can see from these statistics, some of the results companies have experienced in specific situations have been pretty impressive:

- Positive impacts on readers:
  - 10 to 50 percent decrease in reading time
  - 32 percent increase in accuracy in retrieval
  - 13 to 83 percent improvement in initial learning
  - 57 percent decrease in the number of words per document
- Positive impacts on writers:
  - 83 percent decrease in first draft development time
  - 75 percent decrease in document revision time
  - 20 to 50 percent increase in writer productivity
- Positive impacts on organizations:
  - 10 to 50 percent decrease in training time
  - 20 to 50 percent decrease in documentation costs
  - 38 percent increase in documentation use
  - 54 percent decrease in performance error rates
  - 70 percent decrease in questions to supervisors
  - 80 percent decrease in customer service call volume
  - 25 percent increase in compliance rates[5]

USING STORIES TO TRANSFER KNOWLEDGE Stories have been the primary way humans have learned things since we first started to communicate with

---

[5]Statistics published on the Information Mapping Web site: www.infomap.com, November, 2004.

each other. The reason for this is quite straightforward. The story line creates the most efficient contextual framework for knowledge transfer. As Tom Reamy, an expert on knowledge management and corporate learning, says: "First of all, stories are a fundamental means that humans use to structure our worlds. Our brains seem to be wired to easily and almost automatically organize information into stories. The reason that stories are so powerful is that they contain so much in a small amount of packaging. To try to capture all the multidimensionality of stories in simple text without the contextual framework of a story line would expand the story-reading experience to mind-numbing size, not to mention academic jargon overload."[6]

Stories draw people in, painting a picture that makes it easier for the reader to relate to, believe in, and ultimately buy into the underlying message. This is why stories are the best way to change opinions and influence behavior, and why marketing and sales management should encourage the use of user stories and sales success stories whenever possible. This is also why the elements in Value Maps should link to proof stories that validate value and promote the best selling practices.

PowerPoint slides are also a great way to tell reference stories. You can create a simple template for the highlights, and then use statistics and quotes to reinforce the key points of the story and enhance the credibility of the content. Of course, the most powerful way to maximize credibility and knowledge transfer is through audio narrations of the slides in the customer's own voice.

DIVIDING CONTENT INTO SMALLER COMPONENTS   As I mentioned earlier, marketing and sales organizations need to create and organize their content into smaller, more digestible chunks. This will not only make the content more reusable, it will also help improve the transfer of knowledge. As research in structured content has shown, people learn faster and remember longer from short, crisp phrases and things like bullet points and FAQs than they do from long, flowing paragraphs.

---

[6]*KM World Magazine,* Volume 11, Issue 7, December, 2002.

It is important to remember that our entire written communication model has been naturally evolving in this direction. E-mails are a lot briefer and chunkier than memos used to be, and instant messaging extends the sound byte paradigm even further than e-mail. The ultimate extension of this chunked communication model is telephone text messaging, where the screen size limits you to just a few characters. Here, you need to use single letters to represent whole words like "gr8" for "great" and "u" for "you."

Because of the significant benefits of chunking content, I have come to believe that marketing and sales professionals should increase their use of FAQs in all types of marketing and sales content. Not only are FAQs a well-understood structure for both the writer and the reader, but they also accelerate comprehension and improve retention through a technique learning scholars call the "hook and tag."

In layman's terms, questions are provocative. When we read one, our mind creates a deep memory groove for the question called a "hook," as well as a predetermined place to store the answer called a "tag." The real power of FAQs is that humans are naturally inquisitive and genetically predisposed to fill up that tag space. This, plus the fact that FAQs are always perceived as more credible than marketing collateral, is why I tell my clients "FAQs are our friends." I recommend this highly effective knowledge-transfer paradigm be used as much as possible throughout marketing and sales content, not just in customer support content.

IMPROVING THE QUALITY OF PRESENTATIONS

Almost every marketing agency has the skill sets to help their clients develop professionally produced presentations. I believe that agencies can offer considerable value in the right circumstances, but there are also a few common-sense fundamentals that can be applied to the construction of presentation content that will significantly increase its quality and effectiveness from a knowledge-transfer perspective. Studies show that after reference stories, high-quality presentations are what salespeople want most from marketing. Unfortunately, the way PowerPoint has been managed in most companies falls short of these expectations, and it is not just marketing's fault. I have seen plenty of sales presentations over the last several years, and am constantly amazed how often some of the following principles are forgotten and overlooked. Some basic fundamentals to remember are:

- Present a consistent image.
- Increase the percentage of graphics.
- Reinforce graphics with narration.
- Use visuals wisely.

PRESENT A CONSISTENT IMAGE In most sales and sales support organizations, the presentation content that is actually being used is all over the map in terms of look and feel. While all of these companies have created standard presentation templates, I am constantly amazed how rarely these templates are used by the salespeople. Couple this lack of standards with the fact that many new presentations are cobbled together from existing presentations, and it's no surprise that the look and feel of the content often varies from slide to slide. Not only is this inconsistency amateurish, but it also impacts the credibility of the presenter and ultimately the message itself. From my research, I concluded the most prevalent reason standard templates are not used is that, in many cases, they are too restrictive and hard to deal with unless you are a PowerPoint expert.

In my opinion, every company with more than ten sales people should implement a central database for sanctioned PowerPoint content that is managed at the slide level. This centrally managed repository needs to be frequently updated and refreshed so that it is guaranteed to always contain the most current versions of the slides. The database needs to be very easy for salespeople to use so that they go to it each and every time they need to assemble a presentation. This sanctioned PowerPoint content will significantly reduce the amount of morphing and rogue content development going on in the channels and reduce the Total Cost of Content.

INCREASE THE USE OF GRAPHICS A picture is worth a thousand words, and the most effective presentation content makes maximum use of graphics to help the left side of the brain understand and embrace new concepts. As Edward Tufte, Professor Emeritus at Yale and the author of several groundbreaking books on the visual display of information, says, "Graphics is intelligence made visible,"[7] and as Sallie McFague of Vanderbilt concludes, "Images feed concepts. Concepts discipline images. Images without concepts are blind. Concepts without images are sterile."[8]

Nancy Duarte, who runs Duarte Designs in Silicon Valley (http://www.duarte.com), a company that specializes in helping high-tech marketing and sales organizations improve the quality and impact of their presentation material, recently did an inventory of the sanctioned PowerPoint assets of several large technology companies, some of the results of which she shared with me. This analysis showed that the percentage of graphically oriented slides in these companies ranged from a low of 42.1 percent to a high of 95.2 percent. What was interesting to note from this study was the fact that those companies that were generally recognized as engineering driven had a lot less graphic content than those companies having the reputation of being marketing driven.

On the other hand, I often see graphics that are so complex they resemble engineering drawings. The impact of overly complex diagrams and graphics is two-fold. First of all, nobody but the creator can explain the graphic, and second, when confusing graphics are presented by a salesperson, the audience often goes catatonic and tunes the presenter out.

Over the years, it has become apparent to me that the best graphics for selling are conceptual in nature and simple in design with short text labels that allow the audience to comprehend the concept more quickly. This combination of simple graphics and short, easy-to-read textual information improves comprehension. Our brains are designed to work better when more than one sensory channel is activated by incoming stimuli. As a result, the combination of pictures and text activates multiple parts of the brain, getting us to pay attention better and remember things longer.

Simple, conceptual graphics are also more easily embraced by the sales force. One of the tests I suggest for evaluating the effectiveness of a critical

---

[7]Edward Tufte, *Visual Explanations: Images and Quantities, Evidence and Narrative* (Graphics Press, 1984).

[8]Sallie McFague, *Metaphorical Theology: The Models of God in Religious Language* (Fortress Press, 1997).

presentation graphic is whether salespeople can draw it on the back of a napkin when they are talking to a customer over dinner. If they can, I know we have a winner.

REINFORCE THE GRAPHICS WITH NARRATION It's important to remember that PowerPoint presentations are designed to be given in person. In today's environment, however, PowerPoint is being used to communicate complex concepts and information electronically, without a live person there to elaborate. Slides are getting e-mailed and downloaded millions of times each day, and they are viewed by people without anyone there to narrate and explain. Since this practice is likely to continue, it's critical to provide pre-recorded narrations for as much of the presentation as possible.

The combination of graphics and text enhances comprehension and retention, but the addition of audio helps people understand complex concepts and ideas even better. Audio narrations are a great way to explain nuance, plus they add a sense of authority and credibility to the ideas expressed by the content, especially if done by a recognized subject matter expert. If an expert is not available, then use professional narrators to ensure that the production value of the content is the best it can be.

One thing to watch out for, however, is what I call the "talking head syndrome" where people add an actual video of the speaker in the corner of the slide. While this might seem more personal, it usually takes the viewer's focus away from the content, which often dilutes the impact of the presentation. A static picture of the speaker creates the same personal touch without the distractions of a video.

INCORPORATE VISUAL CONTENT WISELY Finally, as part of a quality-centric strategy for visual content, B-to-B companies need to develop a process for deciding what visual content they really need and where they should invest their creative resources. The best way to do this is to start by asking three questions to prioritize which visual content is the most important:

1. How critical is the message we are trying to convey?
2. How difficult is that message to explain?
3. How well can rich media help in the explanation?

FIGURE 17.7 ENHANCING THE DELIVERY

ENHANCING THE CONTENT
DELIVERY EXPERIENCE

As James Gilmore and Joseph Pine conclude in their groundbreaking book, *The Experience Economy,* when you personalize and customize an experience so that it's pleasurable and provides exactly what someone is looking for or needs at that specific moment, then you can't help influencing or even changing that person's beliefs or behavior.[9] This is why one of the four component processes of the Content Optimization Framework focuses on enhancing the content delivery experience, especially from a knowledge-transfer perspective. Enhanced delivery allows salespeople, customers, and prospects to enjoy themselves, absorb the information faster, and retain it longer.

In reality, how well companies rationalize their Sanctioned Content and improve the quality of that content has a great deal to do with the ultimate quality of the delivery experience. Creating more customer-centric content and taxonomies, reducing redundant and out-of-date content, using better writing techniques, and creating more professional presentations all improve the knowledge-transfer experience, thereby helping customers, prospects, and salespeople learn better.

In today's Internet-driven communication environment, the way content is actually delivered will also become a key factor in maximizing the impact on an individual. Delivery will, in some cases, become as important as the content itself. As Marshall McLuhan said in the early days of television,

---

[9]James Gilmore and Joseph Pine, *The Experience Economy* (Harvard Business School Press, 2002).

"The medium is the message," and I believe this is as true today as when he said it. Consider these two key points regarding the Internet:

1. The Internet provides a variety of synchronous and asynchronous communication modes that can impact the delivery experience, and these need to be considered as part of an overall communications strategy.

2. As collaborative technologies expand into every corner of the marketing and sales process, new ways of enhancing the collaborative experience with content will emerge. Smart marketing and sales executives will look for ways to exploit the Web to reduce costs, improve performance, and enhance their competitive advantage.

As I mentioned previously, the ROI from exploiting Web-Assisted Selling can be quite compelling. One of the companies I talked to recently did an analysis of the travel cost and manpower savings they could achieve by implementing an integrated PowerPoint and Web-conferencing system. This system made it easy for sales and sales support people to conduct Web meetings with prospects, replacing some of the face-to-face calls during the early stages of their selling cycle. This company had approximately 1,000 field salespeople and 2,500 sales support consultants. They estimated that replacing even a small percentage of their face-to-face sales and sales support presentations with Web conferences could save them more than $60 million in annual travel costs alone. On top of this, this initiative would also give them 84,000 additional man-days each year that could be allocated toward improving the top line. The total cost of implementing this integrated Web conferencing and PowerPoint management system was less than $4 million per year, including the two to three hours it took to train each sales and sales support person during the rollout. Now that's ROI, and it doesn't even include the significant benefits that come from a more effective needs development and qualification process, more consistent and accurate delivery of the messages, and the reduced administration costs that are a by-product of centralized and more effective presentation management.

I believe that in the coming years, B-to-B marketing and sales organizations will increasingly need to differentiate themselves from their competitors by the way they deliver content. While I certainly don't profess to be a Web design or communications expert, I think there are four principles and best content delivery practices that are somewhat inter-related and build upon each other to pleasantly surprise the audience and help them learn faster. Applying these "Four Cs" will enhance the content delivery experience for salespeople, customers, and prospects, just like the Four Ps I mentioned earlier in this chapter improve the quality of the content.

1. Convenience: There are three aspects of content delivery that measurably increase the convenience for a user and enhance his or her delivery experience:

   • The first is making the content easy to find and access by limiting the number of clicks it takes to navigate to a particular topic or page.

   • The second aspect of convenience is making the information easy to read, which implies using more structured page layouts and optimal typeface and text size for readability on a computer screen.

   • The third aspect of convenience is making it easy for people to use or re-purpose the content in some way, for example, printing out or e-mailing the content to others. In the future, browsers and search engines will also make it easier for people to capture and save small chunks of content for their own purposes. In fact, this technology already exists in a rudimentary form. In 1999, I funded a prototype of a content-clipping function called eNotes. The program allows people to grab small chunks of text and graphics while they are surfing and put them into a "Knowledge Cart" for later use. We put this eNotes prototype on the web as a free, unsupported, downloadable plug-in (http://www.my-enotes.com), which more than 50,000 people have downloaded.

2. Control: Humans want to control things. It's a well-known phenomenon that when people are in control of an interactive medium, they are able to absorb and understand vast amounts of information very quickly, as demonstrated by Figure 17.8. We have all been conditioned over the past several decades to engage electronic media by clicking a control or navigation device. So, when we click a mouse, for example, we are actually preparing our minds to rapidly receive and process new information. In other words, the knowledge-transfer experience is enhanced when we control the clicker.

   If you want to test this phenomenon yourself sometime, just sit next to someone who is clicking through the TV channels with a remote control, and see if you can follow along. Most of us find this enormously frustrating because we lose context and can't follow the rapid change of information. The other person, however, can engage the medium at a much

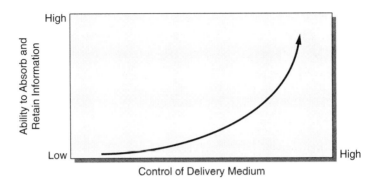

FIGURE 17.8 *THE CONTROL FACTOR*

higher performance level because they are controlling the click. Because he or she is getting an advance warning of a change, that person can process the information faster than we can. This phenomenon also explains why it is so difficult to demonstrate a new software product to a group of people, and why the most effective results occur when the learners control the pace themselves or when the person doing the demo goes excruciatingly slow from his or her standpoint. Another example of this phenomenon is a video game, where each user controls the interaction to create a unique and highly personal experience. The intensity of the interaction is extreme, because this "outside-in" control heightens the players' concentration, enhancing their ability to absorb and learn. Based on these examples, marketing professionals should look at ways to give the user more and more control of the content delivery.

3. Conversation: In addition to control and convenience, some content should be delivered in a more conversational and interactive fashion that more closely represents a one-to-one discussion. A more conversational paradigm does require more componentized and active content, however, which in turn requires more clicks. As such, the technique should only be used judiciously, like when someone needs to navigate through a lot of disparate information quickly to find a specific piece of content. For example, this interactive, conversational paradigm may be the best way to deliver FAQS.

Earlier I talked about how effective FAQs are in transferring knowledge. They can be even more effective when companies use a database to manage each FAQ as an object, including links to all of the other related subjects and FAQs. Instead of having people scroll through pages and pages to find what they want, the conversational model would allow users to jump from FAQ to related FAQ or answer. Since users would control this navigation with a mouse, their knowledge-transfer experience would be enhanced.

More active content combined with a more conversational interaction model could also be used to gather feedback on the content as well as qualification information from customers and prospects. Marketing organizations however, need to become experts at posing relevant and penetrating questions at just the right point in the visitor's navigation process in order to avoid putting off the user. Developing a non-intrusive, pleasing way to engage customers in a substantive Web-based conversation requires a lot of thought behind the navigation model. While this is theoretically possible, I believe we still have a long way to go in this area, which is why B-to-B marketing professionals need to keep on top of new communication and content delivery developments and technologies.

4. Customized: The final aspect of content that will substantially enhance the delivery experience is its customizability. While the concept of customizing is very closely related to personalization, I define these terms differently:

- *Personalization* is when software automatically takes a pre-determined action or delivers pre-determined content to a specific individual based upon some pre-determined rules.

- *Customization* gives the power to the users to assemble the content they select in the way they want.

Enabling customers and salespeople to create the look and feel of a portal, for example, is a great example of how customization enhances the delivery experience and ties a person more closely to the content.

I am also convinced that the effectiveness and productivity of salespeople can be significantly enhanced by helping them customize certain aspects of the sanctioned customer-facing content, while still maintaining a professional look and consistent message. Two techniques emphasize this point:

- The first is the ability for salespeople to create a customized Web portal for their prospects and Internal Champions that helps them answer questions and carry the appropriate messages forward to the other stakeholders in the company. This has several advantages over sending them presentations or documents over e-mail, not the least of which is that more and more e-mail systems are restricting the use of attachments. (Lengthy attachments can carry computer viruses and clog e-mail systems.)

- The second is a new and highly effective communication technique that I call audio-graphic correspondence. This enables a salesperson to follow up a customer discussion with a very short Windows Media or Flash vignette containing some narrated PowerPoint slides specific to the customer's issues. With an easy-to-use narration capability that is integrated with a Web-based PowerPoint management system, the salesperson can customize the vignette by calling an 800 number and adding a personalized audio introduction thanking the customer and introducing the rest of the vignette. This is a much more personal way to communicate than a follow-up e-mail. It creates a greater sense of familiarity and proximity, and it is far more effective in transferring knowledge. These short, self-running audio-visual vignettes are also quite effective in generating interest in prospects, which is why several companies are now using them to get more meetings with the "C" level executives they are targeting.

Of course, no discussion on enhancing the quality of the delivery experience would be complete without talking about Webinars. Lots of companies are using Webinars to generate leads, and quite frankly, most of the ones I have seen were not very effective. I believe you need to look at a Webinar much the same way a producer looks at a TV show—make it so interesting that people would want to tune in next week. Over the last several years, I have collected the following best Webinar practices from people who really get it, like Jim Burns, the CEO of Avitage!, and Gerhard Gschwandtner, the editor of *Selling Power,* who also wrote the Foreword to this book:

- Make sure you rehearse the Webinar.
- Make the topic relevant and provocative. Webinars to cultivate prospects should not be designed like infomercials.
- Include slides with expert narrations to add an aura of credibility and authority.
- The more slides, the better—within reason, of course. I know that we have always been taught to use fewer slides, but that was when the presentation was done in person. Some presentation experts say you should shoot for five minutes per slide when presenting in person but an average of less than one minute per slide for a Webinar. The reason is pretty simple. When you are not present in person, it is harder to keep the audience's attention, but changing slides in a Webinar automatically recaptures the audience's interest.

- Produce it once; hold it several times. By getting the experts to pre-record their portions, you don't need to have them present every time the Webinar runs. Studies show that scheduling a Webinar multiple times gives people options, making them more likely to attend one. Then, each time the Webinar is run, you only need one moderator who is much easier to schedule than all of the experts.

- Finally, by pre-recording the Webinar, you can also offer it on demand. Aberdeen's recent research showed that more than 70 percent of business people preferred on-demand Webinars that they could access at their leisure.[10]

CAPTURING METRICS AND GATHERING FEEDBACK

Two final aspects of the Content Optimization Framework are measuring how salespeople, prospects, and customers use the Sanctioned Content, and proactively capturing feedback and suggestions from the sales channels (see Figure 17.9).

MEASUREMENT AND METRICS The beauty of the Internet is that it was designed from the ground up to measure what is going on. As such, most content management systems include facilities to gather and report on all kinds of different metrics. The challenge, of course, is to focus your

FIGURE 17.9 MEASUREMENT AND FEEDBACK

---

[10]"Best in Class Results From Event Management Technology," report from Aberdeen Group, June, 2004.

attention on gathering the right metrics so that you can discover useful patterns in usage that will help you continuously improve the quality, value, and impact of the Sanctioned Content. To me, these few measurement tactics and best practices make the most sense:

- Measure the overall usage of the various physical and logical components of the finished goods content. For example, compare the use of Power-Point to other forms of content. What most companies find is that Power-Point is far more commonly used and important to the selling process than white papers, brochures, and other content. Of course, in order to collect these metrics, you need to manage presentation media in a more systematic fashion.

- Try to find patterns in usage that correlate with sales success. For example, find out which of the Sanctioned Content the most successful salespeople are using, and publicize this information.

- Measure how the Internal Champions use the content. One of the companies I interviewed for this book created personalized Web portals for their Internal Champions. These portals took them directly to useful content, such as white papers, ROI models, and Windows Media vignettes on their different value propositions. Because this was all done through a Web site, the salespeople could measure how often the Internal Champion and various stakeholders within the customer's company accessed certain portions of the site. This provided valuable insights on what was actually important to those stakeholders.

- Begin to measure the use of critical content at the component and activity level. One of the problems with traditional Web metrics is that you just measure page hits. In the future, however, I believe that more and more people will begin to measure content usage at the component level to answer the following questions:
  - Which PowerPoint slides are the most valuable? To do this, you must measure usage at the slide level instead of at the presentation level. Most enterprise PowerPoint management systems provide this capability now.
  - Which FAQs do people hit the most? If you really leverage the power of FAQs, the answer to this question will tell you a lot from both a sales and self-service support standpoint. As I mentioned earlier, this can easily be implemented by using a database to manage FAQs in a more granular fashion.

- Which content do people print out or e-mail most often? I contend that the more people value content, the more they do something with it. By measuring activities like printing and e-mailing, you can really home in on which content is really valuable and useful.

GATHERING FEEDBACK Perhaps one of the most important design factors of a Value Map, as well as Sanctioned Content, is the inclusion of a simple, integrated feedback process. Such a process will provide salespeople with valuable insights from their counterparts and encourage the sharing of sales intelligence and best sales practices. This is one of the reasons why Value Maps should be built around a structured knowledge model that integrates the value elements with sales insights in a systematic and logical fashion.

I know that getting people, especially salespeople, to share things is difficult, but my experience with WisdomWare taught me that you can use process to change the culture somewhat. Some ways to create an effective knowledge-sharing environment between marketing and sales professionals include:

- Making the feedback process simple to use.
- Making sure every bit of feedback goes to the appropriate person.
- Quickly acknowledging the feedback and thanking the person for it.
- Measuring which content gets the most feedback and who provides it.
- Promoting the importance of feedback and recognizing the salespeople who share their most valuable insights. (What we found with WisdomWare was that this recognition by management was worth its weight in gold.)

Measuring and gathering feedback allows you to see which documents and presentations are used most often. You can then organize the content so that it is easy to access, which enhances the user's delivery experience. Having salespeople as well as prospects and customer rate the content on a scale of one to five stars also helps improve user experience because it identifies which content is the most helpful to the most people.

CONCLUSION

"NASCAR drivers beware! The role of today's chief marketing officer (CMO) is fast becoming one of the riskiest jobs in North America. In the corporate world, where job security is always in question, we have witnessed firsthand the increasing and alarming trend of CMOs going through the revolving door of jobs quicker than other senior executives."

—2004 STUDY BY SPENCER STUART[1]

---

[1]"CMO Tenure: Slowing Down the Revolving Door," study conducted by Spencer Stewart, July, 2004.

The Opportunity for Marketing

IT IS CLEARLY A CHALLENGING TIME for B-to-B marketing executives, and many of their organizations run the risk of being marginalized, regardless of what industry they are in or the size of their companies. Consider these sobering statistics:

- 75 percent of enterprise software companies have recently replaced their VPs of marketing.[2]
- The average tenure of a CMO for the top 100 companies is only 42 percent of the average CEO's.[3]
- Only 18 percent of CEOs are "very satisfied" with their marketing organizations.[4]
- 40 percent of CMOs feel they can't accurately measure their contribution.[5]
- 24 percent of B-to-B marketing professionals believe the stand-alone marketing communications function will disappear within the next 10 to 15 years.[6]

However, thanks to the significant upside that comes from minimizing the waste and lost revenue from the B-to-B Black Hole, this is also a time of extraordinary possibilities for B-to-B marketing executives. Today, more than ever before, CMOs have both the opportunity and the means to redefine the role of marketing in a way that aligns it closer to the revenue

---

[2]Scott Santucci, *Software CEO*, 2003.

[3]"CMO Tenure: Slowing Down the Revolving Door," study conducted by Spencer Stewart, July, 2004.

[4]Survey done by Readex of Chicago, Illinois, reported in www.btobonline, 7/28/2004.

[5]"Management Update: The Evolution of Customer Relationship Marketing," Gartner Group, December, 2003.

[6]Statistics compiled by Robert Schmonsees based on interviews for *Escaping the Black Hole*, Winter, 2003.

generation process, makes it indispensable to the sales organization, and increases its relevance to the enterprise.

As Dennis Dunlap, CEO of the American Marketing Association, says: "The game has changed, and marketing and sales organizations can no longer afford to operate as independent silos. For marketing to increase its relevance in the new economy, it must understand the selling process, align itself with the sales organization, and become a catalyst for improving the quality of the customer's buying experience."[7]

Top line performance is one of the easiest things for CEOs and boards of directors to understand, and increasing sales effectiveness will probably be the single biggest issue they focus on over the next decade. The big question for CMOs is, "Will you take the lead on sales effectiveness, or will members of the sales organization grab the ball and do it themselves?"

The opportunity for chief marketing officers, therefore, is to raise awareness of the perils of the B-to-B Black Hole and begin a dialogue on the sales effectiveness challenge before the Event Horizon becomes a crisis in their companies. They need to convince both the CEO and the CSO that sales effectiveness is part of a much larger and more strategic issue that requires the transformation of both the marketing and sales organizations in order to create a Synchronized Marketing and Sales Ecosystem.

To accomplish this, CMOs must openly acknowledge that their organizations have been part of the problem. They must commit to getting rid of some baggage and embracing significant change in order to make the marketing and the sales channels more effective and productive. They then need to make alignment a central issue, and become the evangelists for integrated processes that increase customer-centricity and drive continuous improvement throughout both organizations—two things nobody will argue against.

As Gartner Group stated in a research report released during the summer of 2003: "Although traditional value-added marketing processes will play a role in the evolution of the marketing function, marketers need to focus their attention on new processes and capabilities. Enterprises must

---

[7]Presentation at the American Marketing Association, Customer Message Management Forum, December, 2004.

find the time to develop and master more advanced marketing processes by improving the efficiency of the marketing function, and by shifting more resources to be better aligned with sales and to produce greater value. By 2007 marketers who devote at least 50 percent of their time to advanced customer-centric marketing processes and capabilities will achieve marketing return on investment that is at least 30 percent greater than that of their peers who lack such emphasis."[8]

The marketing organization, because its numbers are small in comparison to sales, is in the best position to speak in one voice about marketing and sales alignment around the themes of increasing customer focus and continuously improving execution. They are also best equipped to champion new integrated process strategies like the Buyer-Centric Revenue Model and the Value-Centric Communications Model that will enable them to create a Synchronized Marketing and Sales Ecosystem.

Finally, if an enterprise has formally adopted the principles of systems like Six Sigma or the Balanced Scorecard, the CMO can use those management strategies as the umbrella for this transformation effort. But even if there is no previous management commitment to quality initiatives, there are ten techniques and tactics that will help the CMO and his or her organization begin the process:

1. The marketing organization should analyze the impact of the B-to-B Black Hole in their enterprise.

2. They should aggressively reclaim ownership of the value propositions, and start working with the best sales and sales support resources to develop an enterprise-wide Value Map. Driving and ultimately owning the Value-Mapping Process is the fastest way for marketing organizations to demonstrate leadership and prove their strategic value to the enterprise. As such, CMOs should make sure that the Value-Mapping initiative is visible at the highest levels in the organization.

3. They should create a joint task force with sales to define a single, integrated marketing and sales process, and then map that process to the way customers and stakeholders buy their different products and services. As Scott Santucci of Blueprint Marketing told me, "Marketing professionals build credibility when they demonstrate an in-depth understanding of the

---

[8]Research conducted by Gartner Group, Summer, 2003.

complete customer acquisition process. Only then can they determine what kind of collateral and tools are needed to eliminate friction in that process." I contend that marketing organizations have the opportunity and, in reality, the responsibility to play an important role, not only in demand generation but also in stimulating the selling and buying process in each of the other three stages. To do this, they need to better understand each stage and create more effective collateral and sales support tools that reduce the friction between the different stages and accelerate the whole process.

4. Marketing must openly embrace customer- and quality-centric principles like those in the Value-Centric Communications Model, and they must begin cleaning up their existing content and collateral. As Dennis Dunlap, CEO of the AMA, states, "A more systematic and disciplined messaging, content, and communications process not only helps marketers justify their expenditures, it also helps them make the best use of their budgets."[9]

5. Marketing professionals need to adopt a new view of leads. Instead of leads being something they find for sales, they should view them as valuable marketing deliverables that they entrust to sales. This subtlety can make all the difference in the quality of the leads they ultimately produce. The marketing organization must also take visible steps to improve the quality of the information it gathers from prospects. The first step is to classify all the leads sent to sales according to a mutually agreed-upon classification system. This will show the sales organization that marketing is serious about measuring the value they provide.

6. Marketing must also rethink their traditional demand-generation activities in light of the changing market dynamics and new communication model explained in Part I. They must learn how to interact with prospects on a more intimate and conversational level, and how to have one-to-one dialogues with them about the issues that are important. This means that marketing communications professionals will have to develop techniques for asking prospects questions in non-threatening, comfortable ways. This metamorphosis won't be easy, but it's the same transformation challenge that sales organizations faced as they moved from "product selling" to "solution selling" over the past several decades.

7. And speaking of solutions selling, marketing professionals will have to embrace the same solution-selling methodology that their sales

---

[9]Presentation at the American Marketing Association, Customer Message Management Forum, December, 2004.

organizations have adopted, and work with the same training companies to align their marketing activities with that methodology.

8. Marketing professionals will need to embrace the idea that a key part of their role is to help make life easier for salespeople. Their intention should be to help salespeople look as smart as they can to the customers. This may be difficult for some marketing people who have had an uneasy relationship with the sales organization, but if they can't get past this baggage, get them off the team fast.

9. CMOs will need to commit themselves to a higher level of scrutiny and accountability, and come up with better ways to measure the impact of their activities. As Dave Sutton and Tom Kline say in their new book, *Enterprise Marketing Management: The New Science of Marketing,* "Simply put, Marketing must be held to the same standards as any other function across your enterprise. There should be a clear line of sight to how Marketing drives the creation of profits, and Marketing must be held accountable for generating a return on investment consistent with your business objectives."[10] This return on marketing investment should be as specific as possible, and Sutton and Kline provide some good templates in their book to help get marketing organizations started on this critical process.

10. Finally, marketing executives must come to the realization that process and structure is their friend, and it does not limit either their spontaneity or creativity. In fact, I contend that the adoption of systematic integrated processes like the Value-Centric Communications Model will actually enhance marketing's ability to be creative. Furthermore, the additional structure and enhanced focus on the customer through processes like Value Mapping will give marketing professionals a better chance of hitting the ball out of the ballpark on their projects, thereby increasing their contributions to the ultimate success of the enterprise.

If CMOs can step up to these ten challenges, they can be the catalysts for avoiding the destructive effects of the Event Horizon, leading their companies in a direction to escape the B-to-B Black Hole.

---

[10]Dave Sutton and Tom Kline, *Enterprise Marketing Management: The New Science of Marketing* (Hoboken, New Jersey: John Wiley and Sons, 2003).

Index

A

Aberdeen Group, 1, 11*n*, 37, 52, 167, 191
Account ownership issue, 44
The Agenda (Hammer), 113
Aligning, as Leaky Funnel stage, 118
Alignment-centric compensation and recognition, 87
Alignment-centric organization, 84–86
American Marketing Association, 11*n*, 33, 65*n*, 76*n*, 88–89, 173*n*
Assets, misalignment of, 40–42
Audio-graphic correspondence, 190

B

B-to-B Black Hole, defined, 4–11
Balanced Scorecard, 95, 146
Basic Value Map, elements of, 153–154
Best sales practices, as knowledge assets, 41–42
Bitpipe, 51
Blogs, 32–33
Bosworth, Michael T., 68, 88, 137

Branding, 42–44, 49–51, 63–65
"Branding chain", 65
Burns, Jim, 46, 190
Business problems, complexity of, 12–13
"Butterfly Effect", 60–61
Buyer-Centric Revenue Acceleration Model, 119–120
Buyer-Centric Revenue Model (BCRM) integrated lead management and, 123–127
   Leaky Funnel construct and, 116–120
   overview of, 110–112
   Pipeline Radar™ and, 127–136
Buyer/seller power shift, 22–24
Buying process, complexity of, 15–18

C

Callahan, Sean, 64*n*
Cascading Need Phenomenon, 13–15
Chaos Theory, 60
Chief Marketing Officer Best Practices Award for Aligning Marketing and Sales, 89

Cisco, 21, 22

Closings, as Leaky Funnel stage, 118

The Cluetrain Manifesto (Levine, Locke, Searls, and Weinberger), 24

CMM. *See* Customer Message Management (CMM)

CMM Forum, 65*n*

CMO Council, 15, 73, 97–98

Collaborative Strategies, 33

Collaborative technologies, growth in, 32–34

Compensation and recognition programs, 87

Complete Value Map, 154–156

Complete Value Propositions, 24, 57–58, 93, 99–109. *See also* Value Propositions

Componentization, 31, 167–169

Computer-based content development tools, emergence of, 28

Content Conundrum, 77–79

Content management, approaches to, 141

Content-management technology, advances in, 31

Content mismanagement, 70–76

Content Optimization Framework
   basic description of, 142–148
   content rationalization in, 162–175
   and enhancing delivery experience, 185–191
   and improving content quality, 176–184
   metrics and feedback in, 191–193

Content, Total Cost of, 75–79

Control, and content delivery, 187–188

Convenience, and content delivery, 187

Conversation, and content delivery, 188

Cooperman, Stacie, 36

Core Intellectual Assets
   content mismanagement and, 70–76
   manufacturing model for, 100–101
   misalignment of, 40–42
   quality of, 58–61
   Synchronized Marketing and Sales Ecosystem and, 92–93
   in Value-Centric Communications Model, 142–144

Cost, Total, of Content, 75–79

Critical Communications Activities
   misalignment of, 42–44
   quality of, 58–61
   Synchronized Marketing and Sales Ecosystem and, 93–94

CRM. *See* Customer Relationship Management (CRM)

Crossing the Chasm (Moore), 18

The Culpepper Letter, 5*n*

Customer-centricity, 9–10, 54–58

Customer-facing content, 41–42, 73

Customer focus, lack of, 54–58

Customer Message Management (CMM), 88–89

Customer- or needs-focused approach, and value propositions, 45–49

Customer Relationship Management (CRM), 54–58, 62–63, 74–75

CustomerCentric Selling (Bosworth and Holland), 68, 137

Customizability, and content delivery, 189–190
Customization, 189

D

Davis, Andres, 18*n*
Days in stage comparison, and Pipeline Radar™, 133–134
Delivery experience, of content, 185–191
Demand generation, 42–44, 49–51, 117
Demand-generation metrics, 126–127
Dickie, Jim, 9*n*, 88, 133*n*
Direct mail, as marketing channel, 27–28
Discounting, 22
Distribution model, complexity of, 19
Duarte, Nancy, 183
Dueling Product Manager Syndrome, 71, 164
Dunlap, Dennis, 150, 198, 200

E

E-mail, as communication tool, 28
ECM. *See* Enterprise Content Management (ECM)
Ecosystem. *See* Synchronized Marketing and Sales Ecosystem
Enright, Brian, 34
Enterprise Content Management (ECM), 31, 74–75

Enterprise Marketing Management: The New Science of Marketing (Sutton and Kline), 201
eSP Toolkit™, 129–130
Event Horizon, defined, 3–4, 6–8, 83
The Experience Economy (Gilmore and Pine), 185
External behavior, and Pipeline Radar™ reporting, 129–131

F

FAQs, use of, 180–181, 188–189
Feedback
    in Content Optimization Framework, 191–193
    in lead management, 125–126
Flash, and content rationalization, 166–167
Flow factor comparison, and Pipeline Radar™, 131–132
Flow profile analysis, and Pipeline Radar™, 131–133
Four Cs, of content delivery experience, 187–190
Four Ps, of content quality, 176–178

G

Galvin, Joe, 128, 171
Gardner, Alston, 48*n*
Gartner Group, 172, 197*n*, 198–199

Gilmore, James, 185
Glazier, Bill, 10*n*, 15*n*, 73*n*, 98*n*
Glen, T. Michael, 23
Graphics, use of, 182–184
Gschwandtner, Gerhard, 46, 190

H

Hammer, Michael, 113
Harte-Hanks, 63
Hewitt Associates, 52
Hewlett Packard, and study on
    PowerPoint® usage, 29, 72
Holden Corporation, 10*n*, 44
Holland, John L., 68*n*, 137
Hook and tag technique, 181
Human resource assets, quality of, 58

I

IBM Institute for Business Value,
    62–63
Information Mapping, 178–179
Inside-out approach, and value
    propositions, 45–49
Inside the Minds of Leading Marketers
    (Glen), 23
Insight Technology Group, 88
Instant messaging, expanded use
    of, 32
Integrated Knowledge and Content
    Repository, 101, 142–144
Integrated lead management,
    123–127

Integrated pipeline management,
    121–136
Integrated processes, and increasing
    alignment, 9
Integrated sales coaching, 156–157
Integration, of services with products,
    21–22
Intellectual assets
    integrating of, 92–93
    management of, 10–11
    manufacturing model and,
        100–101
    misalignment of, 40–42
    see also Core Intellectual Assets
Internal behavior, and Pipeline
    Radar™ reporting,
    131–136
Internal Champion
    and Cascading Need
        Phenomenon, 15
    in Leaky Funnel stage, 118
    metrics and, 192
    selling tools and, 171–174
    in Value-Centric Communications
        Model, 150
Internal-facing content, 73
International Data Corporation
    (IDC), 89
Internet
    and buyer/seller power shift, 23
    and content delivery, 28, 49–50, 186,
        190–191
    demand generation and, 49–51
    e-mail and, 28
    Web-Assisted Selling, 35–36, 149,
        171–174
    Web conferencing, 33–34
    Weblogs, 32–33
Invisible Cost, of Content, 75–76

J

Johansson, Juliet, 10*n*, 66*n*

K

Kantin, Robert F., 168
Kingstone, Sheryl, 5*n*, 38*n*, 124*n*
Kline, Tom, 201
Klompmaker, Jay, 48*n*
Knowledge advantage, and buyer/seller
    power shift, 23
Knowledge assets, 40–42, 57–58
Knowledge mismanagement, 70–76
Knowledge transfer
    importance of, 53–54
    stories and, 179–180
    in Value-Centric Communications
        Model, 148
Krishnamurthy, Chandru, 10*n*, 66*n*

L

Lead generation activities, 42–44,
    50–51
Lead management, integrated
    approach to, 123–127
Leaky Funnel construct, 116–120
Less is more philosophy, in Value-
    Centric Communications Model,
    148–149
Levine, Rick, 24*n*
Live Meeting™, 33–34
Locke, Christopher, 24*n*

Logical composition of content,
    rationalization of, 169–175

M

Management awareness, increasing,
    88–90
Manufacturing model, for Core
    Intellectual Assets, 100–101
Market-Partners, 129
Marketing and sales
    management mistakes and, 8–11
    nature of, 9
    tactics to improve alignment of,
        85–86
Marketing, challenges for,
    199–102
Marketing collateral, as Sanctioned
    Content, 41–42
McFague, Sallie, 183
McGovern, Rob, 86
McKinsey & Company, Inc., 65, 86
McLuhan, Marshall, 185–186
Message management process, lack of,
    19–20, 45
Message maps, 97–98
Message shelf life, shrinking of,
    24–26
Metrics, 126–127, 191–193
Microsoft, 33
Microsoft Word®, emergence
    of, 28
Misalignment problems, summary of,
    38–49
Moore, Geoffrey, 18
Morphing, of PowerPoint® slides,
    30–31

N

Narration, and graphics, 184
National Institute for Technology and
    Liberal Education, 32

O

Operational processes, and
    Synchronized Marketing and Sales
    Ecosystem, 87–88
Organizational strategy, and
    Synchronized Marketing and Sales
    Ecosystem, 84–86
Outside-in approach, and value
    propositions, 45–49

P

Pareto's Principle, 148
Personalization, and content quality,
    177, 189
Pertinence, and content quality,
    176–177
Peters, Tom, 21
Physical composition of content,
    rationalization of, 165
Pine, Joseph, 185
Pipeline management, integrated
    approach to, 121–136
Pipeline Radar™, 123,
    127–136
Platt, Lew, 53–54
Positioning activities, 42–44, 97–98

Post-commitment phase, of buying
    process, 15–18
Post-sales assessment programs, 22
Power shift, to buyer, 22–24
PowerPoint®
    branding and, 64
    content mismanagement and, 72
    content rationalization and, 166
    Cost of Content and, 76
    emergence of, 28
    growth in, 28–31
    presentation quality and, 181–184
    reference stories and, 180
Pragmatic Marketing, 5n, 38, 48–49, 70
Pre-commitment phase, of buying
    process, 15–18, 23
Precision, and content quality, 177
Presentations, 41–42, 181–184
PricewaterhouseCoopers, 64
Process, and Synchronized Marketing
    and Sales Ecosystem, 87–88
Process Synchronization, 119–120
Processes, misalignment of, 9, 39–40
Product-and feature-focused
    approach, and value propositions,
    45–49
Production, and content quality, 177

Q

Qualifying prospects, as Leaky Funnel
    stage, 117–118
Quality
    of content, 176–184
    in knowledge-transfer experience,
    74–75
    management of, 58–61

R

Racham, Neil, 150
Rationalization, of Sanctioned
  Content, 162–175
*Re-Imagine! Business Excellence in a
  Disruptive Age* (Peters), 21
Readex, 197*n*
Reamy, Tom, 180
Reese, Sam, 133
Revenue processes, integrating and
  aligning of, 91–92
Rich media, 28–31, 165–167
Riesterer, Tim, 106
Roberts, Dave, 92*n*
Rossman, Josh, 21–22

S

*The Sales and Marketing Excellence
  Challenge: Changing How the
  Game Is Played* (Dickie and
  Trailer), 133
Sales and support activities, 42–44,
  69–70
Sales channels
  branding and, 64–65
  in Value-Centric Communications
    Model, 150
Sales coaching, integrated, 156–157
Sales intelligence, restructuring of,
  174–175
Sales/marketing alignment, tactics to
  improve, 85–86
Sales Methodology Experts, 91–92
Sales operations, and redirection of
  marketing resources, 50–51

Sam Whitmore's Media Survey, 51
Sanctioned Content
  cleanup of, 145–148
  growth of, 71–72, 77–78
  knowledge-transfer perspective
    and, 74
  manufacturing model and, 100–101
  as misaligned asset, 40–42
  Synchronized Marketing and Sales
    Ecosystem and, 92–93
  Total Cost of Content and, 75–79
  in Value-Centric Communications
    Model, 142–144
  see also Content Optimization
    Framework
Santucci, Scott, 171, 197*n*, 199
Sarno, Steve, 48*n*
Schlissberg, Hank, 10*n*, 66*n*
Schmonsees, Robert, 197*n*
Schwarzschild, Karl, 3
Searls, Doc, 24*n*
Selling tools
  increasing amount of, 171–174
  as Sanctioned Content, 41–42
"Sensitive Dependence on Initial
  Conditions" concept, 60–61
Services with products, integration of,
  21–22
Shape analysis, and Pipeline Radar™,
  130–131
Shelf life, of message, 24–26
Shimkus, Glenn, 150
Siebel Systems, 89
Singularity, 3
Sirius Decisions, 13
Six Sigma, 59, 85, 95, 146
Size comparison, and Pipeline Radar™,
  130–131
Smart Taxonomy, 101
Solutions, complexity of, 18–19

Solutions-selling movement, failure of, 65–69

Stakeholder/sales process alignment, 170–171

Stakeholders, growing number of, 13–18

Stewart, Spencer, 195, 197*n*

Strategic Proposals: Closing the Big Deal (Kantin), 168

Sutton, Dave, 201

Synchronized Marketing and Sales Ecosystem
benefits of, 94–95
Critical Communications Activities and, 93–94
and integrating Core Intellectual Assets, 92–93
need for, 84–90
revenue processes and, 91–92

T

Teague, Angela, 34

Techniques, to improve marketing/sales alignment, 85–86

Technology Adoption Life Cycle, 18

Telesales, as selling technique, 27

Total Content, 72–73, 75–79

Total Cost of Content, 75–79, 142–144

Total Quality Management (TQM), 59

Trailer, Barry, 9*n*, 88*n*, 133*n*

Training content, as Sanctioned Content, 41–42

Training, for sales, 67–68, 174–175

Tufte, Edward, 182–183

Turbulence, 71–73, 133–135

Two-tier information model, 106–107

V

Value-Centric Communications Model (VCCM)
best practices for implementation of, 145–148
and Content Optimization Framework, 142–144
guiding principles for, 148–150
and Integrated Knowledge and Content Repository, 101, 142–144
overview of, 110–112
strategies and principles of, 140–141
see also Content Optimization Framework

Value Confirmation stage, 118

Value DNA, 56–58, 101–103

Value Mapping™
and basic Value Map, 153–154
best practices for, 157–160
and complete Value Map, 154–156
Complete Value Propositions and, 99–109
elements of Value Map, 151–152
forms for, 153
integrated sales coaching and, 156–157
in Value-Centric Communications Model, 142–148

Value orientation, misalignment of, 44–49

Value propositions
    articulation of, 56–58
    as knowledge assets, 41–42
    misalignment and, 44–49
    see also Complete Value
        Propositions
Ventaso, 11*n*, 76*n*
Visible Cost, of Content, 75
Volume, in marketing and sales
    content, 71–73

Weathersby, George, 81
Web. *See* Internet
Web-Assisted Selling, 35–36, 149,
    171–174
Web conferencing, 33–34
Webinars, and content delivery, 190–191
Weblogs, 32–33
Weinberger, David, 24
Weinberger, Joshua, 63*n*

W

Walker, Leslie, 32*n*
"The War for Talent" (study), 86

Y

Yankee Group, 38

About TEXERE

Texere, a progressive and authoritative voice in business publishing, brings to the global business community the expertise and insights of leading thinkers. Our books educate, enlighten, and entertain, and provide an intersection where our authors and our readers share cutting edge ideas, practices, and innovative solutions. Texere seeks to cultivate, enhance, and disseminate information that illuminates the global business landscape.

www.thomson.com/learning/texere

ABOUT THE TYPEFACE

This book was set in 11/15 Minion.

Library of Congress Cataloging-in-Publication Data

Schmonsees, Robert J., 1947-
 Escaping the black hole : minimizing the damage from the marketing-sales disconnect / Robert J. Schmonsees.— 1st ed.
  p. cm.
 ISBN 0-324-30125-1
 1. Marketing—Management. 2. Selling. I. Title.
 HF5415.13.S3445 2005
 658.8—dc22

                                        2005002894